Philip Mason was born in Harwich, Essex, in 1958. He is a graduate of the London School of Economics where he studied International Politics. After working and travelling in Australia and doing several temporary jobs, he joined the Civil Service in 1984. He has written numerous travel articles and is a keen collector of trivia knowledge.

He lives in Kent with his wife Allison.

D0768353

# WOULD YOU BELIEVE IT?

## Odd Tales From a Weird World

PHILIP MASON

Futura

A Futura Book

First published in Great Britain in 1990 by Futura Publications
a Division of Macdonald & Co (Publishers) Ltd
London & Sydney
1st reprint 1990

Printed and bound in Great Britain by
BPCC Hazell Books
Aylesbury, Bucks, England
Member of BPCC Ltd

ISBN 0 7088 4780 3

Futura Publications
A Division of
Macdonald & Co (Publishers) Ltd
Orbit House
1 New Fetter Lane
London EC4A 1AR

A member of Maxwell Macmillan Pergamon Publishing Corporation

# CONTENTS

# INTRODUCTION

The story was given prominence by the journal of the American Medical Association. An apparently rational student had calmly presented himself to doctors at a Wisconsin hospital and asked if they would be kind enough to sew him back together. He had been trying out a surgical operation on himself and had had difficulty retracting his liver. Could they help? The doctors stitched him up, complimenting him in passing on the professionalism of his technique, before delivering him to a second team of white-coated men who took him off for some serious psychiatric treatment.

The clipping faithfully joined the burgeoning files on the bookshelf, already replete with reports of weird happenings and behaviour from all corners of the world. The man who operated on himself was in good company. There was the venomous snake which died when it chose to bite a drug addict, the Englishmen who lived under his floorboards for eight years to avoid the police, the Indian fare dodger who spent twenty-nine years in jail without trial because the prison system 'lost' him, the Chinese children who could read with their armpits, the Polish man who bequeathed his skull to the Royal Shakespeare Company for use in Hamlet ... and many thousands more, each one a priceless gem of human (or animal) extravagance. This book is a distillation of those accumulated clippings, a ripe harvest of insights into the bizarre side of life on this planet in the latter part of the twentieth century.

Most are humourous, some are sad, many are shocking, a few are simply inexplicable. All though have one common feature. The characters are all ordinary men, women and children (and a few pets). For the most part they have no special talent nor did they seek or have any wish to be cast into the limelight. Most never expected to be noticed or remembered for anything. Fate however contrived to lift them from their happy obscurity for a brief moment of fame or notoriety in this gallery of the curious.

Each of their stories has an unpredictability and a perversity that the fiction writer would not have been allowed to get away with. Take for example the man who tried to commit suicide by cutting his throat. Unusual? Not really. Odd? No. But this one did it by using a chain saw. Now, that's odd. Only the fact that it actually happened can give credence to the tale. No storyteller would have convinced us. Or the dog owner who maltreated his pet by leaving it out for two nights in the freezing midwinter cold. A court convicted him – quite right, you say – but sentenced him to two nights tied up in the same conditions. That's odd. Who could have seriously suggested that as a plot in fiction?

If this volume has any inspiration, it is the old adage that truth is stranger than fiction. In assembling this collection over the years I have come to appreciate the wisdom, indeed the inevitability, of the sentiment. Of course truth is stranger than fiction. Fiction has to make sense. The world out there is under no obligation. And what follows is the clearest testimony to that.

# ONE

# THE UNNATURAL WORLD

'*Good home wanted for year-old Basset bitch. Understands every word I say, but ignores it.*'
Card in Portsmouth shop window, 1979

!

A wild buffalo which had attacked cars around Victoria Falls in Zambia for several days in May 1982 finally picked on the wrong vehicle. It charged a moving train head-on and was killed.

!

A single young moose turned up on Green Island, off the Nova Scotia coast, in December 1982 apparently in response to the only other presence on the island: a lighthouse, whose fog horn biologists concluded must have sounded like a mating call.

!

A sixty-five-year-old farmer was taken to a mental home in Caserta, in Italy, in February 1982 after hanging all his animals – three horses, a dog, a cat and twenty hens.

!

A stray dog which was taken in by a police station in South Africa's KwaZulu homeland in 1981 was named after the homeland's chief, Gatsha Buthelezi, after it had become one of the best guard dogs the Ingwavuna police outpost had ever had. Unfortunately, Chief Buthelezi himself was not enamoured by what he saw as an insult to his authority and registered a strong protest. The South African Police Minister who had overall responsibility for the police station proffered apologies to the Chief and hoped he would accept them in good spirit. But, he added, 'to avoid further possible unpleasantness, the dog has been destroyed'.

!

One of the more unexpected side effects of the Vietnam war was the problem American authorities faced in integrating refugees from Indo-China into urban society. In Utah, officials had to translate the state game laws into Vietnamese, Laotian and Cambodian after refugees were found filling their cooking pots with deer, porcupines, skunks, doves and woodpeckers. In San Francisco, refugees had to be persuaded to forget traditional hunting and trapping skills with which they were rapidly clearing the city's Golden Gate park of its squirrels, ducks – and dogs.

!

In May 1982, a New Orleans appeal court rejected the claim of a convicted murderer who filed a complaint that the police had extracted his confession by draping a boa constrictor around his neck.

!

An ecological maelstrom resulted from the stationing of a unit of Chinese soldiers on a remote island in the South China Sea in 1982. With them, to supplement their uninspiring local rations, they took some chickens which were soon producing eggs – and more chickens, which began to attract predatory rats to the camp. Rat control experts were called in but failed to provide a solution short of getting rid of all the chickens. Not prepared to forsake his eggs, the commander ordered a shipment of cats. These proved scared of the two-pound rats and took instead to eating the rare birds on the island. Dogs were then imported to control the cats which then disappeared up the trees for good, leaving the dogs barking incessantly in the night and fighting each other during the day. A team of 'experts' was eventually despatched from the mainland with orders to effect an ominous 'final solution'.

!

Les King claimed a unique 'fish-in-one' in September 1983 when a wayward drive from the 17th tee on his golf course in Norfolk flew into a nearby river and stunned a two-foot long pike. 'There was a dent on the back of its head where the ball must have hit him', he said afterwards. The pike's fate was to be stuffed and mounted.

!

'Man Bites Dog' – according to a report from Indonesia in April 1986, an enraged villager killed a dog after it had bitten his young son by sinking his teeth into its throat.

!

A procession of caterpillars nearly two miles long and thirty-three feet wide caused chaos in the central Italian town of Fabriano in June 1982. A goods train was derailed when it ran into the mulching parade as it crossed the railway line. 'We hit something mushy and suddenly the wheels started spinning', the driver said.

!

According to British Rail's staff paper, 'Railnews', in October 1980, this remarkable episode occurred on the line between Manchester Victoria and Stalybridge. A man taking his dog for a walk stopped at the automatic crossing barriers at Clayton Bridge to wait for a train to pass. Two cars pulled up alongside, the second one going into the back of the first. Both drivers emerged from their cars and a heated argument began. The man with the dog offered to be a witness but was jostled by one of the drivers who had become highly agitated. The witness tied his dog to the level crossing barrier and prepared to fight back. As knuckles were bared and coats discarded, the train arrived, passed and the barrier went up ... with the dog. The three men forgot their argument instantly and began pushing the tail end of the pooch to prevent it from being throttled. The owner then had to shin up the now vertical barrier to retrieve his retriever.

!

Seville police reported in the autumn of 1983 that an Alsatian dog, seemingly trained by a criminal, was snatching handbags in the city streets.

!

A pigeon race in Taiwan in May 1984 began with over 2,000 starters but only five returned to base. Almost the entire field was trapped in nets on a hillside en route and delivered to local restaurants within an hour of the race's start.

!

According to the *Jerusalem Post* in June 1983, drug smugglers operating on the Pakistan-Iran border had discovered a unique way to avoid capture by customs authorities. They were feeding their camels some of the commodity they were hauling. Tanked up with heroin, the camels were capable of speeds of up to 30mph, far above their normal rate and sufficient to outpace the customs men's charges.

!

Similar properties are invested in the humble grass-hopper when it indulges, according to Ronald Siegel, a researcher at the University of California. He told the American Psychological Association in September 1983 that grasshoppers which eat leaves of wild marijuana plants jump abnormally high, and llamas in Peru became friskier when they chewed the coca plant, from which cocaine is extracted.

!

In December 1982 a fifty-nine-year-old Los Angeles recluse, too poor to buy food, was sentenced to three months' imprisonment for eating his neighbour's dog.

!

A Derbyshire miner's technique of chatting up women – showing them his gerbil – backfired when he tried it on an unsuspecting hairdresser who was driving them on their first date. The gerbil landed in the girl's lap, she screamed and the car crashed into the van in front, causing £1,000 of damage. The fate of the romance is unknown.

!

When artificial inseminators went on strike in the Republic of Ireland in 1981, Irish bulls had to work overtime at the more traditional ways of increasing their herds. Bull owners eventually imposed a ration of forty services a week after two bulls died, apparently from overwork.

!

An Athens pet dealer was jailed for three months in July 1982 for stealing a dog, cutting and dyeing its fur and selling it back to its owner.

!

A venomous snake died after biting a drug addict in a village in central India in 1981. The snake had bitten the middle-aged man during the night and twisted around his leg. When the reptile was pulled off in the morning, it wriggled in agony and died.

!

In twelve years, London investment analyst Robert Beckman amassed a fortune of £100,000 that neither he nor any other human could take advantage of. Even the Inland Revenue finally admitted defeat in February 1985 when it dropped a long battle to claim Capital Gains Tax. The cause of the quandary was William, a twelve-year-old sheepdog who, as a puppy, had a share trading account opened in his name by Beckman. Beckman played the stock market for fun, using William's name to buy and sell shares and stipulating that only William could have access to the profits. The Inland Revenue tried to claim tax liability of £30,000 from Beckman himself. When that failed, it tried to assess William jointly with his owner. No go either. Finally even the intrepid Revenue inspectors gave up. Tax consultants advised that it seemed that while an animal may own property, only humans have the privilege of paying tax.

!

A New Zealand bank thought it had discovered a failsafe security procedure for protecting its cash overnight. It came to an arrangement with the Auckland Safari Park to stash up to $NZ50,000 each night in the tiger's cage. For two weeks the system worked wonderfully until staff could put up with it no longer. Each morning the banknotes returned exuding a foul smell of tiger sweat, urine and ... they didn't like to think what else. The cash had to be sprayed with deodorant before being handed to customers, and ducking under the counter to reach for the aerosol often gave the unfortunate impression to supervisors that a hold-up was in progress. The scheme was hastily abandoned.

!

A shopper in central Warsaw was taken to hospital with concussion in December 1976 after a Christmas goose fell from a six-storey apartment and hit him on the head. He later admitted that he was a poultry farmer.

!

A dog knocked down by a car in Sheffield in 1981 got its own back by running after the driver and, when the car stopped, jumping in and biting a passenger, who needed several stitches in the wound. A vet later pronounced the dog completely uninjured by the accident.

!

Travellers to the remote mountains of Omei in central China received a bizarre warning from the authorities in the autumn of 1982 to beware of marauding monkeys. A gang of three had taken to attacking walkers in the hills. Each was reported to be deformed. One had a hare-lip, another only one eye and the third had missing fingers on its hands. Some sixty separate incidents of monkey muggings had been reported in the previous six months. Visitors were advised to carry extra stocks of food to throw to distract them long enough to escape. A police hunt failed to track the simian rebels.

!

Traffic officer Laurie Weideman got just deserts when he was bitten on the backside by a snake as he crouched in roadside bushes waiting to catch unwary motorists speeding near Durban, South Africa.

!

A mongrel dog betrayed its master when it was abandoned at the scene of a house break-in in Stockport in 1982. The fourteen-year-old burglar was apprehended at his home when police followed the dog as it trotted happily back to his house.

!

A large black monkey caused chaos in central Bombay in January 1983 when it retaliated after its mate had been hit by a motor cycle. It attacked cyclists, bit an ear off a policeman and injured fifteen people before being caught.

!

The *China Daily* reported in June 1981 that 2,000 frogs had fought a fierce battle in a paddy field in southern China. In what may have been a bizarre mating dispute, 'the croaking in the suburbs of Huitong was deafening as hundreds of frogs rushed to join the raging battle. Some frogs were fighting individually while others mounted group assaults.' The battle ended after about two hours when a boy threw a stone into their midst and the frogs fled.

!

Frogs also caused problems in West Germany in November 1984, but this time the law was invoked on their side. A court in Hanau ruled that frogs whose noisy nocturnal lovemaking in a garden pond kept neighbours awake were protected by conservation laws and could not be moved.

!

Abting Bangat, a fifteen-year-old Filipino boy, was swallowed whole by a python he disturbed as he was exploring a mountain cave near his home in 1983. Other members of his tribe killed and sliced open the snake but the boy was already dead.

!

A wild duck took revenge on a hunter in New Zealand's North Island during a shooting trip in May 1985. It dived out of the sky, knocking him out and leaving him with two black eyes, a broken nose and cracked glasses. It killed itself in the process.

!

A 'district rodent operative' called Snowy was sacked by Plymouth health authority when its sleeping habits caused a monumental malfunction to the computer network. The cat found that the computer's hot air vent was ideal for napping, but as the hot air came out so did its hairs which dropped into the vent. They became statically charged and, in July 1984, caused a complete 'downing' of the system.

!

A budgerigar which escaped from its home in Nottingham in August 1982 was returned safely within the hour after telling a schoolboy its name and address.

!

Residents of an apartment block in Bucharest, Romania, successfully applied for the eviction of a neighbour's alcoholic horse which lived in the small, two-roomed flat. The horse, stabled there because its owner said he had nowhere else to put it, was supplied with beer by the bucketful 'to keep it quiet'.

!

Australian farmer Don McKenzie, owner of a property near Benalla, Victoria, devised a spectacularly efficient method of rounding up his sheep. He placed a mirror in his catching pen and reported that it filled promptly and without fail with sheep eager to peer at their own reflections.

!

Police in Lafayette, Colorado, charged Booger, an eight-year-old spaniel bitch, with dangerous driving in February 1980 after the pick-up truck it had been trying to park damaged a fence. Booger's owner, Michael Wilson, explained, 'I have to work the brake and accelerator. Anyway, she's a rotten driver.'

!

The veterinary service in Ghana reported in August 1981 the birth of a creature that was half-human and half-goat. It was born dead in Accra, had a human face, goat's ears and four legs.

!

Park officials in London's St James's Park had to remove two pelicans from the stock of birdlife in the summer of 1981 following complaints from passers-by using the park as a lunchtime retreat that the birds' predatory habits were a little off-putting. The pelicans had taken to snapping up pigeons, gobbling them down whole and then regurgitating them to make way for more food, such delicate actions usually being performed in front of sandwich-munching office workers.

!

During the Falklands conflict, a crack team of under-cover operatives were landed on a remote beach to gather intelligence. Before reaching the top of a ridge they heard voices. 'We couldn't understand what they were saying and assumed they must be Spanish-speaking,' Captain Nigel Bedford explained, recalling the story in July 1982. The group of 148 Commando Forward Observation Battery took evasive action and remained pinned down until dawn. 'We lay there completely motionless and hardly daring to breathe, only to discover in the morning that the "voices" were penguins.'

!

A bird's nest found at the top of a 60 ft lightning mast at Gatwick Airport in 1982 had been constructed from tough wire, broom bristles and nylon cord. It took wire-cutters to remove it.

!

When eighty-four-year-old Hilda Diggden, who had spent a lifetime caring for cats and had taken dozens of strays into her house, died in Stoneham, Massachusetts, in November 1982 her remains were eaten by her pets. Cats living in the house attacked police officers who tried to recover the body. 'The body was in a semi-skeletal state,' one officer reported 'It was one of the roughest things I've ever seen. They were literally feeding off her.'

!

Mrs Margaret Brown was awarded £5,000 damages in the High Court in November 1982 after being knocked down by a car as she tried to save a rabbit from the same fate. The judge said that she had been partly to blame for the accident which occurred as she was trying to chase the rabbit off the road. She had tried to flag down the oncoming car but admitted to closing her eyes at the crucial moment. 'I turned and closed my eyes because I didn't want to see the rabbit being squashed,' she said. The car hit Mrs Brown, and the rabbit.

!

A French woman was seriously injured when her poodle accidentally pushed her out of her fourth-storey flat window in Strasbourg on Christmas Day 1982. Claudette Reinert was about to take the animal for a walk when it excitedly jumped up, knocking her backwards through the open window.

!

A West German woman caused £25,000 worth of damage when she made the mistake of taking her moody cat with her on a shopping trip. Leaving it in the car as she shopped in Wuppertal, it was in high dudgeon by the time she returned. As she drove off it bit her, causing her to lose control of the car which rammed a stationary one and demolished a sausage stand which dragged down a fish-frying stand with it, burning an assistant with boiling fat. A passer-by fainted and the woman's car was a write-off. The cat was uninjured.

!

A Masai tribesman was arrested in February 1983 for attacking a stuffed lion in the Ministry of Tourism offices in Nairobi, Kenya. The man broke the glass case containing the exhibit and began strangling it. He explained that his brother had been killed by a lion and he was extracting revenge. He appeared to think that the lion in the foyer of the building was merely docile and would be an easier target than one in the wild as it was clearly used to Man and would be easier to take by surprise.

!

A year-long search for a bird thought to have been extinct for 130 years ended for a British naturalist Dick Watling in Fiji in May 1984 when it fell on his head. The bird, MacGillvray's petrel, was lured at night from the sea using flashlights and recordings. After crashing on his head, the bird was examined and let free.

!

In May 1982, Chong Shing-Keung threatened to bomb a Hong Kong oil refinery unless a $HK75,000 ransom was paid. He delivered several hundred homing pigeons, each with a small money bag strapped to it, to the company's offices with instructions for the bags to be filled. Unfortunately for Chong the simplicity of the wheeze was not lost on the police. They merely followed the birds in a helicopter and they were led straight to Chong's hideout.

!

Lawrence O'Dowd was fined £100 by York magistrates in November 1984 for using threatening and abusive language and behaviour likely to occasion a breach of the peace. The court was told that O'Dowd had said 'miaow' to a police dog. Sgt Taylor had considered the miaow to be threatening in the circumstances.

!

In February 1985, RSPCA officers received complaints about an eighty-year-old Maidstone lady's pets. When they investigated, they found her living with a total of thirty-seven dogs in her unlit and unheated two-up, two-down house. All the animals were removed for their, and her, safety.

!

A fitting story to end this look at Man's relationship with the animal world:

In June 1985, David Reynolds, a game warden in a nature

reserve near Durban, South Africa, allowed himself to be gored by a charging black rhinoceros rather than shooting it because it belonged to an endangered species. He suffered battered legs and his thigh was ripped open, 'but it's what the job is all about', he said.

# TWO

# ONE IN THE EYE OF THE BEHOLDER

'*A product of the untalented, sold by the unprincipled to the utterly bewildered.*'

Al Capp, cartoonist, defining abstract art

'*If it sells, it's art.*'

Frank Lloyd, art dealer, 1978

**!**

Scottish artist William Turnbull won second prize of £3,000 for his blank canvas painted white at the John Moores art exhibition in Liverpool in 1978. Called 'Untitled No 9' it could be hung either way the artist said. 'The back of the picture has "top" written on two sides because basically both experiences are correct. It is not gravitationally oriented,' he explained. The first prize of £6,000 went to an equally esoteric work entitled 'A painting in Six stages with a Silk Triangle'.

**!**

Joseph Ramsauer won the second prize at the 1982 Rock Island Fine Arts Exhibition in Iowa. He received $400 for his work which comprised an adhesive bandage framed neatly on a large sheet of white paper. He admitted to being surprised by his success.

!

In October 1980 Dublin Corporation's cultural committee voted by 8 to 5 to purchase an apparently blank canvas from an American artist for £21,000. The artist, Agnes Martin, said that the work was executed in 'transparent materials', described as graphite, gesso and Acrylic. One councillor who opposed the purchase told the committee that it would be the same as 'going into a restaurant, ordering dinner and getting an empty plate'.

!

An untitled work by American artist Cy Twombly was sold by Sotheby's for £50,000 in December 1982. It consisted of six lines of looped scribblings on a blank canvas five feet by seven. One commentator said that the merit of the work was its 'particular fluidity'. The buyer remained anonymous.

!

In 1961, Henri Matisse's painting 'Le Bateau' was put on exhibition in the New York Museum of Modern Art. Forty-seven days later it was noticed that it had been hung upside down.

!

Maureen Gledhill of Liverpool bought an abstract work for £70 from a local artist in October 1983. She later discovered that the pretty, dappled composition had been executed not by the artist, Ernie Cleverley, but by Pablo, his pet duck, after an accident in the workshop. The new owner was not impressed but failed in her attempt to return the painting and get her money back. The artist was unrepentant. 'It could be worth a fortune anyway. The duck is a natural.' The picture was later later destined to be sold for charity in Canada as one of the world's worst paintings.

!

The Arts Council paid £7,000 in 1981 for a work which featured, amongst other things, a tray full of animal droppings. The creation was the work of two Norfolk artists and was their view of Nature's yearly cycles. Constructed mainly out of sawn pine logs tied with twine, it incorporated old farm tools, rusty horseshoes, an old green mouldy boot, dead and decaying leaves and carefully laid out piles of horse manure and rabbit droppings. The exhibit was all part of a show called 'Continuous Creation' at the Serpentine Gallery in London's Kensington Gardens. Comments in the visitors' book ranged from 'oversimplified' to 'bullshit'.

!

French sculptor Fernandez Arman stacked sixty old cars encased in concrete into a 59 ft high sculpture in Jouy-en-Josas in central France in 1982.

!

A 'contemporary art' exhibition at the Pompidou Centre in Paris in 1981 included a work by Swedish artist Goran Hagg: a model of a bare-chested woman that showered those who looked too closely with water from its mouth. According to the catalogue, the model posed 'intricate questions relating to the relationship of art and reality'. The exhibition also included six stuffed ducks rotating slowly beneath an ultra-violet light and accompanied by squawking noises.

!

The Scottish National Gallery of Modern Art paid £23,000 in 1982 for a work by sculptor Cesor Baldachini – a 6 ft block of rusting car parts crushed into shape by a hydraulic press, entitled 'Compression 1966'. The gallery defended the purchase, feeling that the 'sculpture' would help people understand twentieth-century artistic thinking and make people question the way art is developing'. It was an aspect of the waste of modern society, a 'twentieth-Century totem' it opined. A local scrap merchant seemed to agree. He immediately offered to create the same effect – for £6.

!

A Venice art school teacher, who dressed up as a male sexual organ during the city's 1982 carnival, was arrested for offending public decency. Giorgio Spiller, a 'behavioural artist', contested the charge on the grounds that there had been no problem when he dressed up as a female sexual organ during the 1981 carnival.

!

The Tate Gallery faced scathing criticism in 1976 when it put on show Carl Andre's sculpture comprising 120 fire bricks. The Gallery had seen a photograph of the work four years before, but when it offered to buy it Andre had already returned the bricks to the brickyard and got his money back because he could not find a buyer. So he bought some more, crated them up and sent them off to the Tate. The Gallery defended its purchasing policy, saying that it was seeking to be 'more adventurous'. A Labour MP offered to construct a tableau of saucepans from the Commons' canteen and give any proceeds to party funds. The Tate's response is not recorded.

!

When Nottingham's new Royal Concert Hall was officially opened in 1982, guests were somewhat perplexed by an unsightly appendage to the building. Officials were on the point of contacting the builders to remove the remaining scaffolding when a senior member of the Hall's authority confirmed that the tangled and twisted tubing was in fact a piece of sculpture purporting to symbolise the lace trade.

!

The Arts Council paid £600 in 1984 for a sardine tin in a steel bath tub. The sculpture, purporting to represent the sinking of the Belgrano in the Falklands war, was described by the Council as 'arresting and mysterious'.

!

Visitors to the Tate Gallery in January 1985 mistook a demonstration by 280 art students against spending cuts for an avant garde exhibit.

!

In January 1984, Ainsley Huskisson of Peterborough successfully wrote the Lord's Prayer four times on the back of an ordinary 12½p stamp.

!

In 1981, the Arts Council gave £2,500 to a composer whose chief claim to fame was playing the hosepipe. Trevor Wishart invented the instrument which he called a Dapplephone. He had previously used scrap cars as instruments and had composed 'Air on a Car Bonnet'.

!

A thirteen-strong artistic troupe from Barcelona called La Fura Dels Baus (literally translated as 'The vermin of the sewers') introduced London audiences in the winter of 1985 to the 'Auto-destructive school of theatre'. In each performance, the 'artists', dressed only in G-strings, sledgehammered three motor cars to pieces, demolished brick walls and doused each other in paint. The theatre director of the Institute of Contemporary Arts which hosted the show called it all 'exciting and ironic'. Not exciting enough for the ICA to pay for the extravaganza. The show went on courtesy of the city of Barcelona who coughed up the cash.

!

For six months in 1980, French artist Jean Verame painted a valley in the Sinai desert red, blue, black and yellow. He covered an area of 70,000 sq ft before international conservationists demanded a halt to this example of 'conceptual art'.

¦

Gunther Demnig, an assistant in the Cassel School of Art in West Germany spent twenty-four days in 1980 walking the 800 kilometres from Cassel to Paris pushing a self-invented contraption which left a thin chalk line in its wake. Despite the rain having obliterated most of the residue by the time he reached his destination, he claimed to have completed the longest work of art in history. He said he planned a longer line next, from Cassel to London, this time in blood, and perhaps one in petrol across the Atlantic to the Museum of Modern Art in New York. More immediately he would be unravelling a ball of string en route from Cassel to Venice.

!

In Guayaquil, Ecuador, the statue of revered poet Jose Joaquin Olmedo is not all it seems. When the town wished to raise the monument to their artistic hero they discovered the cost of a new statue to be prohibitive. A local foundry however offered them a second-hand statue of Lord Byron cheap. They bought it, made some changes to the face, erected it in the town square and put Olmedo's name on the pedestal.

!

The mysteries of art are only exceeded by those of human behaviour. When the 'Mona Lisa' was stolen from the Louvre in 1911, and went missing for two years, more people went to stare at the blank space than had gone to look at the masterpiece itself in the previous twelve years.

!

From the Artists Newsletter of November 1984 comes this piquant announcement: 'The conference on "The Art Britain Ignores" which was to have been held at Huddersfield in September was cancelled through lack of interest.'

!

Qi Xing, a Shanghai textile worker marked the centenary of Karl Marx's death in 1983 by engraving the full text of the Communist Manifesto on to a piece of ivory the size of a matchbox. He squeezed over 20,000 Chinese characters into the 2 in by 1 in block.

!

An Old Bailey judge in a celebrated art forgery trial in 1979, examining one of the alleged forgeries concluded, 'I fail to see how this could possibly have been mistaken for the real thing. The trees are woolly, the houses are woolly, the people are woolly, even the sheep are woolly.'

!

An artist, whose name is not recorded, who specialised in paintings of storms at sea, had some of his work exhibited at a show at St Ives. A schoolgirl who studied the paintings intensely and was then introduced to the artist, exclaimed with deep sympathy, 'You really had terrible luck with the weather.'

!

For the struggling artist, any crumb of comfort is rewarding, as this overheard exchange during an art show testifies: 'Did you sell any of your paintings?' 'No, but I felt quite encouraged; somebody stole one.'

!

This notice from a Wiltshire Women's Club newsletter will evoke empathy from any amateur artist: 'Mrs —, who took up painting only three months ago, exhibited portraits of club members and still lives.'

!

From an American book called *The Drawings of Dali* comes this author's acknowledgement whose wording might have been better: 'The publisher wishes to thank Mr and Mrs Reynolds for permission to draw heavily on their extensive Dali collection.'

!

# THREE

# THANKS FOR THE MEMO RE

'*It's like watching an elephant become pregnant. Everything's done on a very high level, there's a lot of commotion, and it takes twenty-two months for anything to happen.*'

President Franklin D. Roosevelt,
on the workings of the State Department

'*Prayers have to be notified on the correct form or they will not be processed.*'

Church notice, Phoenix, Arizona, 1979

!

All bureaucracies, in order to be efficient, so they say, find the need to adopt what they call 'standard operating procedures'. But as is evident here it is precisely these pigeon-holing approaches which make the office worker inflexible to the unexpected. Take as an example the note sent by a finance company: 'We thank you for returning the completed application form, but regret that you have omitted to give us the name and address of the employer with whom you are self-employed.'

!

The builders of a dry ski slope in Perthshire were told by the local council in 1981 to 'colour it green' so that the appearance would be in tune with the landscape.

!

A Middlesex hospital catering memo distributed during reorganisation in 1981 read: 'Patients wishing to order pancakes should tick the box marked "Apple flan and custard" and likewise patients ordering jelly and ice cream should tick the "Fruit salad" box.'

!

A Birmingham garage owner who in 1973 bought a 23 ft glass fibre statue of a gorilla to stand outside his used car sales business was refused permission by the Registrar of Business Names to call his enterprise King Kong Kar Kompany on the grounds that it might have been construed as having Royal patronage.

!

This announcement was appended to a notice board at a prestigious seat of learning in the north country in 1979: 'Members of the Admissions sub-committee who yesterday received a yellow sheet of paper are asked to imagine that it is pink.'

!

The United States' Internal Revenue Service guide to Federal Income Tax includes this paragraph of advice: 'Illegal income such as stolen or embezzled funds must be included in gross income.'

!

The Edinburgh tax inspector wrote in 1981 to advise one family: 'The late Mr X is not liable to Income Tax from the 5 April 1980 and therefore it is not necessary for him to complete any Income Tax forms.'

!

Generosity indeed, but not all countries are so forthcoming. The family of a Geneva man who died at 4 am on New Year's Day 1986 received a tax bill for 10 Swiss centimes (about 4p) as his tax liability for the year.

!

The passion for balancing the books leads inevitably to the pinnacle of bureaucratic neatness. In 1982, Haringey Council in London sent a bill to a local church for 10p, representing two year's rental of a directional sign – in an envelope bearing a 12½p frank.

!

Wesley Zubkow, an American airman stationed at Bentwaters base in Suffolk, returned home in 1982 after his tour of duty in Britain. He thought he had cleared all his bills, but failed to reckon with Eastern Electricity. Shortly after arriving home he received a letter telling him that he had been overpaid in his last rebate by 1p, and asking him to repay it forthwith. Zubkow settled the demand with the helpful assistance of his erstwhile neighbour in Suffolk who agreed to pay the Board herself.

!

After working for just four years before retiring, Carla Owczarek did not think she would be entitled to a pension. After being inundated with forms and reminders, she eventually sent off an application in July 1982. She promptly received her first Giro cheque – for 8p a fortnight. 'The stamp costs more than the payment', she kindly wrote back, 'let alone the paperwork at the DHSS'. A compromise was agreed. DHSS would send £1.04p every six months.

!

In a blitz to recover £4.5 million in unpaid rates, the Welsh Water Authority contacted some 20,000 of its customers in October 1983. Peggy Carey, a widow in Penarth received a letter threatening court action unless she settled her outstanding debt of 1p. The demand arrived by first class post at a cost of 16p.

!

In the days when there were telegrams, the Post Office's efforts to improve the service led to the issue of leaflets explaining that in future all words with ten characters or more would be counted as two words. Thus, 'Love and congratulations' was four words in length, unless of course, it advised, one wrote 'Loveand congratulations' – that would be only three. Said a Post Office spokesman, 'We are in the process of streamlining the service, and this rule facilitates the mechanical handling.'

!

A disabled pensioner was threatened with prosecution by Stroud district council in September 1983 if he did not pay a rates bill of 1p. The Council apologised after blaming a computer error.

!

The American tax collecting agency, the Internal Revenue Service, announced in 1984 its arrangements should the Bomb drop. It may waive penalties for filing late returns, it decided, but Post Offices still functioning would supply survivors with emergency change of address cards.

!

A Leeds mother whose electricity was cut off in November 1981 because she owed £500 in bills went to the Social Security office for help – and was given £5 to buy a torch. A DHSS spokesman said the torch was offered because when such bills were not paid 'we have a duty to make alternate arrangements'.

!

When a gas explosion destroyed the Middleton family's home in the Derbyshire town of Loscoe in July 1986, an East Midlands Electricity Board official arrived to pull the meter from the rubble. In addition to receiving a bill for the amount used up to the explosion, the Middletons were charged £147.92 excess for damaging the meter.

!

In a clean-up drive in 1980, the city commission in Fort Lauderdale, Florida, passed a strict law banning obscenity in books, magazines and records. It then discovered that under the law, its own wording was obscene and could not be published.

!

In similar vein, the Tasmanian government once censored its own list of censored publications. The state's attorney general said he stopped publication of the 2,000-item list because he was 'so disgusted' with the titles.

!

During a power crisis in New South Wales in 1981, the Electricity Commission rejected a request from the firm Polly and Son, which had asked for exemption from power cuts due to heavy demand for their product. The company made candles.

!

The Saffron Walden and Dunmow joint reorganisation committee was finally wound up in 1974 when a group of members met for five minutes with the specific and only purpose of closing down the committee. The committee had continued in existence long after others in Essex had been disbanded because at its previous meetings there had never been enough members present to take any action.

!

A working party was set up in Southampton University in 1981 to report on ways of reducing and streamlining the University's committee structure. The party failed to arrange a date for its first meeting because all its members were fully occupied with other committees.

!

Prompted by a forest fire in 1976, the parish council in the Hampshire town of Ringwood announced its intention to establish an emergency committee to deal with any future crisis. It reported in 1980 that the committee was 'now starting to take shape'.

!

British Rail seemed to be afflicted by the same disease. It announced in 1980 that management and unions had just agreed that because Christmas Day fell on a Saturday in 1976, all staff working on the railways at that time should have an extra day off in the forthcoming year.

!

A Lancashire local paper reported this major administrative upheaval in 1976: 'The tourism, recreation and amenities department of South Lakeland Council is to undergo a fundamental change – in future it will be known as the amenities, recreation and tourism department.'

!

The executive committee of the Torbay Sport Advisory Council decided at a meeting in 1978 to appoint a sub-committee to investigate ways and means of setting up proposed sub-committees.

!

In 1980, Brighton Council set up a Performance Review sub-Committee to improve town hall efficiency and cut costs. Councillors then voted that one of the best ways of saving money was to axe the sub-Committee.

!

A Greater London Council circular in 1981 announced the earth-shattering news that 'As Miss —'s official title is Controller of Transportation and Development, the Department's name has now been changed from Transport and Development to Transportation and Development Department'.

!

When the Department of the Environment applied restrictions under the Ancient Monuments Act on excavations in the grounds of Fulham Palace in January 1983, allotment holders were informed that they would now require permission to retrieve their onions, leeks and carrots if they grew more than eight inches below the surface. A DoE official confirmed that separate application forms would be required for each article to be 'excavated'.

!

The small man's battle against bureaucracy was exemplified in 1981 by this plaintive letter in a national newspaper:

'In April alone, my company has received from the Inland Revenue:

- —One copy of 'Income tax year 1979–80: notice of assessment and statement of tax underpaid or overpaid';
- —One 'Income tax assessment for the year to 5 April 1980';
- —One 'Tax return form for 1981–82';
- —One 'Tax return guide for 1981–82' (in twelve closely printed pages);
- —Two copies of 'Employer's annual statement, declaration and certificate';
- —Two copies of 'Return of expenses payments and benefits etc to or for directors and higher-paid employees, year ended 5 April 1981';
- —One leaflet explaining (not very clearly) how to deal with 'Return of expenses payments and benefits etc';
- —One 'Form to be filled in if a director or employee has not received any expenses payments and benefits etc';
- —One leaflet 'Deduction of tax and national insurance contributions from wages, salaries etc';
- —One 'PAYE changes which affect employers immediately';
- —One 'Employer's stationery requisition';
- —One 'PAYE: employer's permanent record of employees (optional)';
- —One 'Year ending April 1982: PAYE tax tables

**34**

and deductions working sheets';
—One 'Income tax: employee for whom no code notified to employer';
—One 'P15 coding claim';
—One 'Notice to employer of employee's code';
—Two copies of 'Form P60';
—Two 'Deductions working sheets (new)';
—One booklet 'Employer's guide to PAYE' – in sixty closely printed pages.
—Six reply paid envelopes.

This list does not include forms, correspondence and so on from the other two tax collecting organisations, the Department of Health and Social Security and the VAT office of the Customs and Excise.
The company has *one* full-time employee!'

!

After months' wait, John Bright finally heard from his local council in October 1983 that his crumbling seventeenth-century summer house in his Warwickshire garden was listed as an historic building and thus qualified for a restoration grant. The news was very slightly tempered by the fact that the whole thing had blown down in a gale a few days before.

!

A newsheet headlined 'Let us get Greenwich back to work' was circulated by the Borough Council in 1981 to all local firms urging them to use local suppliers of goods and services. It was printed in Bedford.

!

The backbone of the bureaucratic machine is the 'expert', which has been suitably defined as consisting of 'X', the unknown factor, and 'spurt', a drip under pressure. No doubt experts were engaged in these exercises:

A peak hour traffic survey in Belfast in 1981 caused one of the city's worst traffic jams. A council spokesman said that the aim of the survey was to find ways to reduce road congestion.

!

The Greater London Council decided to conduct its own traffic census in 1982 – on a day when the Underground was on strike and traffic on the M11, already nose to tail for miles, was impeded even more by a team of council workers stopping motorists to ask how they thought London's traffic could be improved. A number of the answers were said to be 'unpublishable'.

!

During the drought of 1976, a press notice from the Inland Waterways Association helpfully contributed to the public's understanding of the crisis: 'On most canals, the primary cause of water shortage was found to be insufficient supplies of water.'

!

The Department of Employment played a similar game in its October 1976 edition of *Employment Gazette*: 'The increase in male unemployment for men between 1966 and 1972 can be fully explained by the almost continuous fall in male employment in this period.'

!

The manager of the Department of Health and Welfare in Boise, Idaho, initiated his own time and motion study as part of a cost-cutting drive in January 1981. At odd intervals seven times each day, Robert Jensen blew a whistle, at which all secretaries had to stop work and fill out a form saying what they were doing before the whistle interrupted them. The 'Random Moment Time Study' involved a 14 in long form which took fifteen minutes to complete. Secretaries called it 'insulting', 'degrading' and 'disruptive'. After two months of operation, the Department decided that the best way of improving efficiency was to abandon the survey.

!

A claimant at a social security office in Brighton in 1980 was confronted by a clerk with masses of paper and files representing a considerable investigative operation. He was informed that he had been overpaid by £6 more than thirty years ago in Belfast and they wanted it back.

!

The Southern Electricity Board issued this notice to its larger customers in 1974:

'In consequence of the metrication of the fuel cost adjustment in the Bulk Supply Tariff, the fuel adjustment in your tariff has been changed to metric weights and calorific measures. The unit prices are subject to an increase or decrease at the rate of 0.00051p for supplies taken at High Voltage and 0.00054p for supplies taken at Low Voltage for each new penny (a half or any greater part of a new penny being treated as a new penny) by which the monthly cost of fuel per tonne in the month before the month of account as charged to the Board at a gross calorific value of 26,000 kilojoules per kilogramme of fuel by the CEGB for the supply of electricity in bulk either rises above or falls below £4.25 per tonne as the case may be.

For all practical purposes, this change can be taken as having no effect on the amount of the fuel adjustment.'

!

As a cost-cutting measure, the office of the Premier of the state of Victoria in Australia issued a directive in 1982 that all press releases from the State rail service, VicRail, would henceforth be on white paper instead of the usual pink paper. The saving on the 12,000 copies of VicRail releases each year? $1.80. But the Premier's Department ignored its own directive ... by putting it out on blue paper.

!

At the opening ceremony of Maidstone's bottle bank in 1980, the Mayor declared that 'waste in any form is something that no council should accept'. He then proceeded to spray a bottle of champagne over the town's new amenity.

!

A Wigan couple who had fostered forty-seven children in the past were told by their council in July 1981 that they were no longer fit to adopt children because their marriage was too happy. The council explained: 'It would seem from the interviews and reports that both of you have had few, if any, negative experiences when children yourselves, and also seem to enjoy a marital relationship where rows and arguments have no place.' A child growing up in such circumstances would not be sufficiently exposed to 'negative experiences'.

!

VicRail is a standing joke for the hapless commuters of Victoria, as we shall discover in due course, but it is not only its train services that confuse its customers. One who went to a station in the eastern suburbs of Melbourne in 1982 to send some veterinary pathology samples to the University found that the charge was $2.20, or $3.30 sent 'Fragile'. 'But just quietly,' the station man said, 'we send the fragile stuff with the ordinary mail anyway.' On enquiring the reason for the 50% extra charge, the customer was told, 'Well, I've gotta stamp 'em "FRAGILE" twice.'

!

Section 4 of the Irish Republic's Road Traffic (Insurance) Disc Regulations 1984 stated: 'Every Insurance disc shall be in the shape of a rectangle.'

!

The United Nations General Assembly's Special Committee Against Apartheid's Sub-Committee on the Implementation of United Nations Resolutions on Collaboration with South Africa is known for short as UNGAS-CAASCIUNRCSA.

!

When R W Brady got on the Automobile Association's computer, it added an initial making him R G W Brady. He altered this on one of its forms: 'Not G, just R W.' His membership card arrived duly altered, made out to Mr G Just R W.

!

An unfortunate limitation on the number of characters per line led the mailing section of *Computer Talk* magazine to address Analyst Programmers simply as Anal Programmers.

!

In 1980, the Post Office sent letters to more than five million people without telephones explaining why their bills had been delayed. A spokesman blamed a computer error.

!

The complacent notion of all operators that the computer can do no wrong led the US Army in August 1985 to send a $28,560, seven-ton ship's anchor to a base 1,000 miles inland in Colorado. A clerk had wanted a $6 headlight but typed the wrong code into the computer ordering system. It had not occurred to anyone to query the order.

!

On police insistence, Blackpool borough council spent £56,000 on measures to protect Conservative Party delegates to the annual conference in 1985. In return, the Government told the council they intended to lop £100,000 off their rate support grant for overspending.

!

The day after villagers at Pill, near Bristol, in December 1983, celebrated the resurfacing of Upper Myrtle Hill after a three-year battle with Avon County Council, South West Gas dug it up.

!

The planning application list before Monmouth district council contained in 1984 this item relating to a cottage in Abergavenny: 'Rebuilding existing lean-to extension which collapsed when being altered to comply with building regulations.'

!

When seven departmental heads of a large Birmingham company were invited to attend a one day seminar on 'Delegation' in 1979, five of them sent their deputies.

!

When callers to the visa department of the Czechoslovakian Embassy got no reply, they telephoned the consular department to ask why. They were told that although the visa department was open from 10 a.m. to 1 p.m., the telephones were never answered because the officials were too busy. The telephones, it was explained, were answered only between 2 p.m. and 4 p.m., when the visa department was closed.

!

Disabled residents in Weymouth complained to their MP in 1981 that they were being unfairly discriminated against when seeking assistance on rehousing. The local Disabled Persons Resettlement Officer could be found in the Job Centre at the top of a flight of stairs. There was no lift.

!

The Monopolies Commission was obliged to ask the Government in 1981 to extend its deadline by another three months to complete a study – of the efficiency of bus companies and why they often failed to meet their timetables.

!

In March 1981, Liverpool Council discovered that it still employed three gas lamp lighters and a mate eight years after the city's last gas lamp was extinguished. The city's Chief Engineer admitted 'the men have been under-employed'. While not completely idle (they used to sort out gas appliances in school kitchens and council houses), they did however 'sit around' for 95 per cent of their day. 'Naturally, with there being no gas lamps they do not have a lot to do,' he added. The cost to Liverpool's rate-payers was estimated at £250,000.

!

In April 1981, civil servants in the Italian Foreign Ministry staged a 'strike in reverse' and carried on working after they should have finished for the day. The work-in was mounted to back the demands of colleagues elsewhere in the civil service who had walked out in the more traditional way. Foreign Ministry union leaders rejected similar tactics on the grounds that 'professional habits' would lead to most of them turning up for work anyway. 'It is psychologically difficult for them to arrive at a form of protest which harms Italy's interests', a union official explained. The work-in lasted until 2 a.m., during which time neither diplomats nor office staff took meal breaks.

!

In December 1981, the High Court in Patna, India, ordered the release of a man who had been in jail for twenty-nine years awaiting trial. Ramchandra Kashiran had been arrested in March 1953 for travelling on the railway without a ticket. Prison authorities lost his papers during transfers between jails and hospital where he was treated for depression during his first few months in custody. Kashiran, who always thought that the state's case was being prepared, languished forgotten. When civil liberty lawyers managed to get him bail, he told them, 'I had started to think it was all taking rather a long time. I won't mind if they send me back to prison, I've rather grown to like it'.

!

The Court of Account, France's highest public watchdog which supervises the country's nationalised industries, revealed in its 1983 Annual Report that working in the French National Centre for Scientific Research had been a physicist who went on strike in 1969. His absence was not noticed until 1981. In the same report, it revealed that the cost of coal production in Gare was £395 per ton. It was being sold for £66 per ton.

!

The last case pales into insignificance in comparison with the Pentagon's lackadaisical approach to the management of public funds. In August 1983, auditors discovered that the US Air Force had paid $1,118.26 (then about £736) for a plastic cap to fit under a fold-away stool to prevent wobbling during flight. The Pentagon later found that it had been paying the exorbitant price for the caps for the past four years before anyone had noticed. The estimated production cost of the caps was 26 cents each. The auditors' appetite whetted, the next two years of investigation uncovered a glut of financial horror stories, including the expenditure by the Army in May 1983 of $252,000 to instal new boiler systems and improve car parking facilities at several bases which were due for demolition; the purchase by the Navy of $8.8m worth of uniforms it did not need; the Army's purchase of new batteries for $76m even though existing ones could adequately be recharged with existing equipment; and the unquestioning way in which the services bought individual items for grossly inflated prices: $748 for a pair of Air Force pliers, $436 for a Navy hammer, $7,600 for an Air Force coffee pot and $640 for a Navy toilet seat.

!

# FOUR

# COMMERCIAL BREAKS

'*Due to internal reorganisation in order to improve deliveries and our service to clients, the delivery of units is presently being delayed by four to five weeks.*'

Harrogate building firm announcement, 1982

'*Ejection seat tester ... small amount of travelling involved.*'

Army vacancy list, 1979

!

In early 1982, senior executives of an Australian pharmaceutical company in Sydney received with astonishment reports from an outback chemist shop in Western Australia that sales of its piles ointment were at record levels. Month by month they continued to rise. Clearly there were major problems out there, but the medical services reported nothing unusual and stockists in the neighbouring town showed normal sales patterns. So intrigued did Head Office become that a rep was sent out to see the chemist and discover the reason. The pharmacist, seemingly unconcerned, told him the secret. The ointment was emptied out and rebottled as nappy rash treatment. 'My customers think it's my own remedy and it sells like hot cakes,' he revealed. And the applicators? the rep asked. 'I use them for golf tees,' he confided.

!

An initially successful example of free enterprise in Moscow came to Western ears in October 1982. With used bottles commanding a 15p refund, there is considerable incentive to tidying up the streets of the capital. A twelve-year-old called Sasha, whose dog, Jack, kept raking up bottles from beneath park benches and bushes hit upon the commercial possibilities. The two went out each night looking for empties, and before long the whole family was involved with mother storing them and grandfather taking them back to the stores while Sasha was at school. By the end of the first month they had made half the family's normal monthly salary from the scheme. Unfortunately, the enterprise fell foul of that ubiquitous Russian character – the snooper. Neighbouring families reported them to the police. An over-keen Jack was the main problem. Being rewarded with a sugar lump for every bottle retrieved, he took to harassing any passer-by who happened to be carrying a bottle and roaming the parks to snatch not so empty bottles from the hands of drunks.

!

In 1981, the Government-based Alkali Inspectorate named a factory at Aberavon, in South Wales, the country's smokiest factory. It made smokeless fuels.

!

As a mark of its reliance on the beef industry, the town council of Point Reyes, in California's cattle country, decided in January 1986 to adapt the town clock. It now moos, instead of chimes, every hour.

!

Financial acumen was not a natural gift for a twenty-five-year-old Indonesian rickshaw driver called Molyono who made the discovery of a lifetime in December 1983 when he found sixteen gold bars in an old wooden box he had bought for firewood. He did not, however, know what they were. After selling two for 55p each as fishing weights, his father took the remaining bars to the local police who put a value on them of £25,000. The police, who concluded that the gold had probably been mislaid by smugglers, were not surprisingly unsuccessful in tracing the purchasers of the other two bars.

!

Mark Stancapiano's novelty message business collapsed in ruins in August 1985 when he introduced the Rambo-gram, delivered by a Sylvester Stallone look-alike, complete with combat fatigues, cartridge belts and automatic gun. On his first outing in Buffalo, New York, he got lost. As he was passing the Erie County Courthouse, he popped in to see if a policeman could direct him. The ensuing panic caused a major police alert with scores of officers descending on the area and surrounding the building as reports of a gun-toting maniac flashed across the city. A bemused Stancapiano was overpowered and arrested. He was later charged with threatening behaviour and disorderly conduct.

!

The British Tourist Authority's brochure circulating in Spain in 1985 was emblazoned with a picture of Sir Francis Drake.

!

The American motor giant Chevrolet failed to appreciate the local dimension when it ventured into the Latin American market with its new model, the Nova, in the early eighties. After disappointing sales, executives realised that No Va in Spanish translated as 'it does not go'.

!

Business owners in the hard-pressed West Midlands hit upon a scheme in 1982 to reduce running costs. They stripped the roofs off their factories when production was temporarily halted by the recession. This exempted them from having to pay rates on the grounds that rates could only be charged on buildings capable of being used, and it was successfully maintained that a factory without a roof was not so capable.

!

When Bournes, the Oxford Street store, announced in March 1983 that it would be closing down the following August, it had already been holding a closing down sale for over a year. The extra six months created what was thought to be a record for any sale.

!

A New Jersey trader won the ultimate contract in June 1983, to supply Saudi Arabia with 300 tons of sand. It was for use in a water treatment plant in Jeddah, and Saudi sand was proving too coarse for filtering.

!

A Post Office advertising campaign backfired in 1982 when 3,000 companies in the Midlands received 'an explosive package from the Royal Mail' – packages designed to look like parcel bombs complete with mock sticks of dynamite advertising Datapost and Expresspost services. The scheme was hastily scrapped when recipients claimed the whole idea was in bad taste. At least one company had been alarmed enough to call the police. The Post Office later admitted that 'perhaps the wrong approach had been chosen' to get their message across.

!

The Legal and General Insurance group opened a new office block in Melbourne, Australia in December 1981. As a publicity stunt, two pretty girls stood outside offering passers-by $5 credit vouchers. All recipients had to do was deposit the voucher in an account, which could, they were assured, be closed straight away if they wished, with the $5 to keep. Seventy-five per cent of those approached refused to take the vouchers on the grounds that they did not believe someone could be giving them something for nothing.

!

After a spate of serious rail accidents in the summer of 1985, most of which were subsequently deemed to have been caused by driver error, French railways dropped their unfortunate advertising slogan: 'You can go all the way with your eyes closed'.

!

The Isle of Wight Tourist Board admitted shortly after its 1984 guide had been published that the happy couple pictured with their four children on the cover had been divorced five years before. The photograph was seven years old.

!

The art of advertising brings out the best in human idiosyncrasy. There are the adverts which reach heights of wit:

A road sign erected just outside a small Californian town in 1981: 'Precision Instruments Co: 104 yds, 2 ft, 9 ins ahead.'

Slogan for an Ayr camping company's sale in 1983: 'Now is the discount of our winter tent.'

A Brighton opticians in 1983: 'If you don't see what you want, you've come to the right place.'

A London flower barrow, 1978: 'Your fuchsia is in my hands.'

A Brighton classical record store in October 1976: 'There are only 48 Chopin days to Christmas.'

There are those which have tried to be a little too clever:

A St Albans dry cleaner's guarantee: 'Should you feel we have failed you in any way, we will be only too pleased to do it again at no extra charge.'

A Hampshire store in 1981: 'These gifts will not last long at these prices.'

A Southampton Indian restaurant advertising in 1983: 'Once you try our Northern curries, you will never want to try any other curries again.'

An Edinburgh travel agency in 1979: 'Please do us a favour and go away.'

A dry cleaners in Cala Mayo, Majorca in 1980: 'Drop your trousers here for best results.'

London street market, 1979: 'Invisible hairnets, five colours.'

The rest you just simply don't understand:

On a bottle of chilli sauce bought in Delhi: 'This is your guarantee of genuine product. Do not buy bottle if this label is not on it.'

A Hong Kong tailors, in 1984: 'We are prompt, no matter how long it takes.'

!

A Chesterfield bus garage was brought to a standstill in September 1980 in a dispute over which member of staff should go on a training course. One maintenance engineer refused to go and was suspended, leading to a walkout by colleagues. The course was a management–union liaison exercise in industrial relations.

!

The Chinese *People's Daily* reported in September 1981 that workers at a steel mill which was about to be closed because of inefficiency stripped the plant and sold machinery at knockdown prices. It was the largest income the mill had ever earned.

!

Picketing miners who stood round-the-clock duties outside a power station in Halifax during the strike in February 1974 withdrew their guard after a week when a kindly local policeman told them that the station had closed down three years before.

!

Pickets during the 1979 dock strike discovered their mistake a little sooner. Arriving in the early hours to lay siege to Immingham docks, they set up their brazier and placards in front of the large iron gates. Only when dawn came did they realise that they were picketing the town cemetery.

!

Work on completing Melbourne's futuristic Arts Centre came to a halt in May 1982 for seven weeks because of a demarcation dispute between painters' and carpet-layers' unions over who should lay the carpet cladding on the walls.

!

Taunton's Brewhouse Theatre was overwhelmed when it advertised in August 1983 for a supporting role in its production of Tom Stoppard's comedy *The Real Inspector Hound*. The key part was that of the corpse which lies perfectly still on centre stage for over an hour of the performance. A real 'live' corpse was needed as dummies proved unconvincing enough. A twenty-eight-year-old unemployed forklift driver later beat fifty other applicants for the £4.68 per show job.

!

At the height of Idi Amin's reign in 1978, the Government of Uganda approached the World Bank to fill a key appointment in the nation's financial world. The Bank contacted an anonymous Englishman, telling him he had a prepaid cablegram of twenty-four letters with which to reply. His reply ran precisely:
'HA HA HA HA HA HA HA HA HA HA HA HA'.

!

Judge Robert Belew of Fort Worth, Texas, ruled in June 1985 that American Airlines had not acted unfairly in sacking Robert Cox, a trainee steward, because he did not smile enough at passengers. The judge agreed that the airline policy of requiring a 'friendly facial expression' was necessary in the competitive airline industry.

!

It was reported from Bangkok in December 1987 that a man who had walked 600 miles from southern China to Thailand to find a job had been arrested for illegal entry.

# FIVE

# HELL ... O!

*'Please enjoy your flaming dinner.'*
Invitation to barbecue, Tokyo hotel, 1981

*'For guests who are coming back when dining room is over and want food, the night porter will make things hot for them.'*
Istanbul hotel, 1980

!

Since the Tower of Babel, Man's need to communicate with his fellow earth dweller has been bedevilled by the necessity to understand other languages. The problem of translation has been to convey the nuance behind the sentiment as well as the words themselves. Shortcomings in this department are responsible for the *double entendres* illustrated above, which are, in the great scheme of things, harmless and of no lasting consequence. Where it matters however such deficiencies are not necessarily overcome with any greater panache. At the highest levels of international intercourse, the simultaneous translator plays the key role in international (mis)understanding Failure on their part could lead to diplomatic incidents, broken relations or even worse. The following is a selection of recent contributions to the cause, extracted from translations at the United Nations in 1981. The word in brackets is what should have been translated into the other working languages rather than that mistakenly broadcast:

'The United Nation's Secretariat's fear (sphere) of competence ...'

'... create a society in which men could enjoy the fruits of their neighbour (labour) without interference.'

'Support for the depraved (deprived) people of that territory.'

'... would give the eighteen-nation committee a new impotence (impetus).'

'Parliaments (armaments) were no longer considered the best guarantee of national unity.'

'Great successes have been achieved in the Ukraine in combating various diseases. The number of deaths (beds) has increased by 280 per cent.'

'The predator (creditor) must not be deprived of his rights.'

'The working group had a number of naughty (knotty) problems to consider.'

'In pre-revolutionary Russia, immortality (immorality) had been high.'

!

As if there weren't enough problems for Europe, similar difficulties of language confront the EC which, in 1983 (before Greece, Spain and Portugal joined) was spending £62 per page on translating documents into the six working languages at an overall cost of £100m a year. Half of the running costs of the European Parliament (£180m in 1986) was devoted to translation requirements where it was estimated that a one word amendment to a resolution costs £350 to process. Not only is it taxing on the purse but the results can burden the diplomatic skills too. During a meeting in 1985, a Greek interpreter brought proceedings to a standstill when he translated the effect of a small dispute as 'throwing a Spaniard in the works'. A visiting Polish delegation was reported to be calling for more troops in Warsaw. The cultural committee had been discussing visits of theatrical troupes. When a British delegation described their task as being like 'paddling a canoe shooting rapids', it came from the German interpreter as 'shooting rabbits'. The delegation were promptly wished good hunting.

!

During the 1979 general election, commentators pointed out the suitability of the main combatants' names. Incumbent Prime Minister, James Callaghan, we were told, in Dutch would be roughly 'kaale haan' which translates as 'poor old cock'. Margaret Thatcher, meanwhile, in French would be Margaret Chaumeur. When pronounced it bears a remarkable similarity to 'chômeur', which means an unemployed person.

!

The *Indonesian Observer* provided a quixotic view of British life when it reported the resignation of John Stonehouse in 1976. In recording that he had gone by the traditional method of applying for the Chiltern Hundreds, its effort read that he had applied for the post of 'steward and bailiff of the three hundreds of children'.

!

An Australian journalist in China in 1981 unwittingly caused some embarrassed coughs when he described his position as rather like a pianist in a brothel, ancillary to the main action. Unfortunately, his Mandarin interpreter translated the word pianist as a rather similar sounding appendage of the male anatomy.

!

Such misunderstandings are not confined simply to faulty translations. There is the, no doubt apocryphal, story of the woman who called at the BBC's Overseas department and asked for the Urdu section. The commissionaire directed her to a ladies' hairdresser – for an 'airdo. Then there was the naval officer who received a verbal message from the cockney rating informing him that he was to report to Ari Jaba. Having searched unsuccessfully in his atlas for this exotic posting, he discovered, on picking up his written orders, that he was going to Harwich Harbour.

!

Not all misunderstandings may pass without serious consequence. In July 1983, sixty-nine passengers on board an Air Canada Boeing 767 had a lucky escape when the plane was forced to crash land halfway through their flight from Montreal to Edmonton when it ran out of fuel. Investigators later discovered that it had only been half fuelled because someone had confused imperial with metric measures. Instead of leaving Montreal loaded with 22,300 kgs of fuel (or 49,060 lbs) it left with only 22,300 *lbs*. The airline blamed recent changes in refuelling practices for the error.

!

Other forms of communication are equally prone to using wrong measures. On 21 May 1981, the presenter of BBC Radio 3's 'Morning Concert' mistakenly played 'The Cunning Little Vixen' by Czech composer Janacek, at 45 rpm instead of 33 rpm. Nobody noticed until the piece finished eight minutes earlier than it should have done.

!

Radio 3's advance into the world of electronic acoustic music in late 1984 was somewhat marred by its broadcast backwards of a piece by one Margaret Sambell. Fortunately, no-one except the composer apparently noticed.

!

The media's coverage of sport is perhaps the greatest gold mine for examples of otherwise normal people committing verbal harakiri. In Australia, every winter's Saturday afternoon sees ranks of sports commentators from Melbourne's dozen or so radio stations converge on football grounds to carry live coverage of the city's Aussie Rules games. The sport, a cross between rugby, basketball and all-in wrestling, is fast and furious with few breaks from the action. It therefore causes, to an unusual degree, the difficulties of all 'live' broadcasters, that of spouting forth first and thinking about it later. The following immortal lines from recent seasons illustrate a disease of almost epidemic proportions:

'The Ablett brothers are hard to tell apart, although one has a beard.'

'It's a long kick by Miles.'

'It's Merrett. It's Duckworth. It could be Clarke …'

'South Melbourne played better in the rain than they do in the wet.'

'Foschini nearly had his head pulled off – Featherby goes to ground and picks it up and boots it forty metres down the ground.'

'Carlton defeated Melbourne by a solitary ten points.'

'Garry Wilson is the only player on the field to have kicked two goals – the rest all coming from players who have kicked one.'

'The reason Lewis hasn't been doing much at centre-half-forward is that he is still sitting on the inter-change bench.'

'Strachan is a left-handed bouncer and a right-handed kicker.'

'I don't want to individualise – but you must be happy with the form shown by young Cordner.'

'He's kicked it high, right up towards the air.'

'It rained for an hour just a moment ago.'

'The ball has bounced on a bare patch of grass.'

'If you look around at their side, they're just not there.'

'Hawthorn's Terry Wallace burrowed through the pack and came out untouched, although he copped a few knocks.'

'When he's not there his presence is really felt.'

'He does it so easily when he does it, you wonder why he doesn't do it all the time.'

'Kourkoumelis – he passes to a player who isn't there.'

'It's a very good poor kick by Tipper.'

'All the 'O' players are playing well – O'Sullivan, O'Donnell, McGlashen, Dickson ...'

'He's not very fast, but by gee, he's quick.'

'Most of the majority of players do it.'

'If you could put Michael Moncrieff's head on that bloke's shoulders he'd look just like Michael Moncrieff.'

'I'd say that's pathetic football at its best.'

'There weren't too many best mans on the ground today.'

'How he doesn't get killed more often, I don't know.'

'He was the first to get there first.'

**!**

The affliction is not confined to football. Cricket commentators are also renowned for their descriptive oddities. One might have thought that there would be no excuse. All that time spent waiting for something to happen would, one thinks, be ideal for ensuring that the utterances are refined and eloquent. Far from it. All that waiting evidently addles the brain. The sudden shock of action on the field hurls the commentator from dazed mental slumber to the need to say something, which, they regretfully muse afterwards, 'sounded all right at the time'. Like these:

'Laird has been brought in to stand in the corner of the circle.'

'I've seen batting all over the world ... and in other countries too.'

'Hookes was out without scoring for a duck.'

'Mudasser was going to hook that ball but it was suddenly on to him slower than he expected.'

'For those who don't understand what bowling in the blockhole means, it is when the ball is pitched right up into the blockhole.'

'It won't matter if he doesn't score, as long as he keeps getting singles.'

'Julian Wiener is a tall, athletic fair-haired blond.'

'It's a lovely day at the Gabba ground – most of the people are shirtless and quite a few are footless too.'

'It was really not a memorable innings but I think he will remember it for a long time.'

'And in comes Bob Taylor, looking very distinguished with his grey hair, which you can't see because it's completely covered by his helmet.'

'And Allan Lamb is out caught – just as he was nearing the middle of a great innings.'

'The chances are that we may see the best of the morning in the early part of the day.'

'The crowd are standing on their feet.'

'You can't help feeling that England's big mistake was allowing the West Indies to score quite so many runs.'

'What a truly amazing catch that was by Bruce Yardley, low to his left. The ball literally never left the ground.'

'The Trinidad Oval is exactly what its name implies. It's completely round.'

'Had he cut it, it would have been a piece of cake.'

!

These sports are not the only cause of broadcasting mayhem, as the following media bloopers testify:

'... and later, the radio doctor will be along with her spot.'

Capital Radio continuity, 1979

'Aircraft accidents seem to be a great hazard for us while we are on the road.'

Don MacClean, *Star Special*, Radio One, 1980

'Now, Muhammed, that's a popular Christian name, isn't it?'

Interviewer of Muhammed Ali, 1980

'And this lad, with all the world in front of him, finished fifth.'

David Coleman on Steve Ovett, Montreal Olympics, 1976

'In a little while, we hope to have the pole vault over the satellite.'

David Coleman, Montreal Olympics, 1976

'We are now going over to our reporter who accompanied the march on one leg.'

BBC News, 1981

'She (Mrs Reagan) got into the bath, and he (Mr Reagan) jumped into the shower and while they bathed, Mr Carter threw in the towel.'

AAP-AP newsagency, reporting Reagan election victory, 1980

'Here are just a few bus cancellations in case you missed them.'

BBC Radio Brighton, 1983

'There's a smile on Willie Thorne's face, with his nose just in front.'

David Vine, snooker 1985

'That brings broadcasts on Radio 3 to a close today, although in fact it is already tomorrow.'

Continuity, 1985

'And now, just before 'The Sinking of the Scharnhorst', attention all shipping ...'

BBC Radio 4 continuity, 1984

'The road has been affected by severe flooding – traffic is reduced to a crawl.'

BBC Radio 2 traffic news, 1984

'Police have asked motorists not to make even essential journeys.'

BBC Radio 4 announcement, 1984

'I'm joined now by Trevor McDonald, who is down at the summit.'

Channel Four News, 1986

'It's all about AIDS, and you can get it by phoning this number ...'

Radio 1 DJ, 1987

!

The Press can also get it wrong. This correction appeared in a New Zealand newspaper in 1981:

'Mai Thai Finn is one of the students in the programme and was in the centre of the photograph. We incorrectly listed her name as one of the items on the menu.'

!

A computer failure which knocked out all typesetting equipment at *De Morgen*, one of Belgium's leading newspapers, on 9 December 1986 ensured that the following day would enter into newspaper history. The thirty-two pages of the 10 December edition were written entirely by hand. The only photograph that day showed journalists busily scribbling their copy in their best handwriting. The edition quickly became a collector's item and was sold out by lunchtime.

!

In July 1986 Malaysia's Telecommunications Minister, Datuk Leo Moggie, laid on a press conference in Kuala Lumpur to publicise the connection of the country's one millionth telephone subscriber. When he dialled to talk to the lucky customer he got a wrong number.

!

He got through eventually. The same could be said for the postcard which, it was reported in June 1983, had just been delivered to its destination in Brighton. It was stamped with a 3d stamp and franked in 1965. The Post Office was unable to explain the eighteen-year delay.

!

# SIX

# MISSED DEMEANOURS

'*Can criminals become useful members of society? Yes, if you give them time.*'

Graffiti, Yorkshire, 1979

'*If the person who stole a radio from here on Monday will get in touch with us, we will give them the guarantee card.*'

Notice, Wembley shop window, 1976

!

The first thing we are supposed to learn about crime is that it never pays. That has not stopped some valiant attempts to prove the point:

Six Peruvian gunmen used a light aircraft in February 1979 to rob an isolated farm in the mountainous north of the country. The robbery netted a haul of £500. The cost of hiring the plane and buying fuel was considerably higher than the loot.

!

A County Tyrone man who tried to fiddle his electricity meter in January 1982 turned the key the wrong way, and received a bill for £600, ten times the normal amount. A court then fined him £25.

!

Three gunmen who held up the manager of a fried chicken shop in Sydney in 1982 ran off with the paper bag he was clutching. They escaped with his Chinese takeaway lunch.

!

Thieves who ransacked the Scottish highland mediaeval fortress of Dunbeath Castle near Wick in December 1982 escaped with a haul of armour, swords and shields supposedly dating from the Middle Ages. The American owner confided to police investigating the robbery that in fact the artefacts were Spanish-made replicas of twentieth-century origin.

!

Christopher Byard picked the wrong time to break into the boot of a Mini in Halesowen in May 1982 to steal the spare wheel. Two policemen were still inside their car, unseen through the frosted up windows. He was jailed for two years.

!

Police were not too concerned by the theft of a postman's delivery bag in Long Eaton in February 1984. Most of the letters it contained were telephone bills.

!

Thieves stole a £150 security grille from the White Space Art Gallery in Islington, north London, in November 1985. They left untouched thousands of pounds worth of abstract art.

!

The Sydney *Sunday Telegraph* recorded in 1974 the story of a Melbourne woman who had bought a cardigan from the Myers chain store. She found that it did not fit and decided to take it back. As she drove to the shop the next day, she had the misfortune to run over a cat. A little distressed, she took the cardigan out of her Myers plastic bag and put the cat in, planning to bury it. In the Myers car park she put the bag on the car roof while juggling other parcels, forgot about it and headed off to the cardigan counter. A few minutes after she remembered about the cat and was returning to the car when she saw another woman making off with the bag. The thief was found stretched out later on a coffee-shop floor.

!

Phil Cockayne, a Walsall burglar alarm specialist had £3,500 worth of property stolen from his home in May 1985 while he was out on a job ... installing burglar alarms.

!

Jewels worth £175 were stolen from the offices of the BBC *Crimewatch* programme in March 1986. They were to have been used as samples from a burgled jewellers being featured on the programme.

!

A visitor to Belgium from the Gambia discovered in August 1984 that honesty was not necessarily the best policy. Arriving at Brussels airport, Manju Turay was routinely asked by customs officials whether he had anything to declare. 'Yes,' he replied, 'fifty-five pounds of cannabis.' He was later jailed for three years.

!

Jimmy Simmond, a prisoner at Highpoint, in Suffolk, was recaptured thirty minutes after scaling the security fence in the summer of 1985. When he tried to hitch a lift to the nearby village of Little Bradley, the first car to stop and oblige was driven by detectives being called to the prison.

!

A New York mugger tried to hide from his police pursuers in July 1985 by climbing into a rubbish compressor. The machine was switched on while he was still inside. The police later reported that he had been 'crushed into a little ball'.

!

Criminals are not the only ones to suffer. Victims, of course, have a pretty torrid time too:

A Brisbane man out for a quiet stroll in February 1982 established some kind of record by being mugged three times by a total of ten people in less than an hour. The anonymous man met four women in a bar and had gone with them to a nearby park with a crate of takeaways. After downing some, the women downed him and snatched his wallet. He gave chase but lost them. He returned to the park to find three men helping themselves to the remaining beers. He remonstrated with them. They beat him up and fled with the cans. Somewhat worse for wear, he staggered in search of a police station, asking directions from another group who promptly beat him also and stole his driving licence. He finally made it to South Brisbane station.

!

A Bristol man who was mugged in the St Paul's area of the city in June 1986, losing his wallet and cash, was robbed a second time on the way to the police station to report the attack. When he told the second mugger of his plight, he was relieved of his shoes and socks. The police returned the victim to where he had parked his car, to find it had been stolen too. Said a police spokesman, 'One way and another, it just wasn't his day'.

!

In March 1984 a New York woman, whose telephone credit card had been stolen in a mugging two months before, was warned by the telephone company that her bill for February was ready and would soon be delivered ... by truck. It duly arrived, in five crates, 2,578 pages long, recording over 15,000 domestic and international calls, made at the rate of more than 500 a day. The total came to almost $110,000 (£75,000). After negotiation, the company agreed not to hold her liable.

!

A commuter who understandably wishes to remain anonymous suffered his car being stolen twice from Peterborough station car park in 1979. He finally bought an old banger for the station trips and fitted a safety lock. A week later thieves stole the lock but left the car.

!

A Seattle court sentenced Rocky, a bull terrier, to death in July 1983 for his part in a mugging. The prosecution claimed that Rocky obeyed his master's order to attack a man. The dog was later reprieved when his real owner claimed him.

!

Ray Gleason, deputy sheriff in Port Huron, Michigan, chased two suspected bank robbers for three miles despite having been shot between the eyes by one of them during a raid in January 1985. After apprehending them, he went to hospital to have the bullet removed.

!

Two nights before he was shot dead during a robbery in December 1981, Miami fish merchant Rafael Gonzalez dreamed it would happen. He told friends and described his attacker. His dream led to the arrest of the alleged killer, a former employee.

!

Raids on banks and similar institutions form, of course, the most direct approach to procuring ill-gotten gains. Nevertheless, some still hope that a spark of ingenuity will pay dividends:

The Japanese reverence for obeying authority almost let twenty-three-year-old Shuichi Tamai carry off an audacious raid on the Matsuyama City Agricultural Cooperative in May 1979. A telephone call purporting to come from the local police alerted the branch manager to an impending crime prevention drill. A 'robber' would soon be arriving. Two million yen was to be prepared and handed to him. The drill would test police in the area who were ignorant of the plans. The robber duly arrived, appropriately masked and carrying a knife for effect. The money was handed over and he made his getaway in a car. Akira Nagase, the branch manager, phoned the police back to proudly tell them the drill had gone perfectly. The police coolly replied that no drills were being carried out that day. Tamai was later picked up. Another Japanese trait, thoroughness, had come into play. An employee had taken down the number plate of the getaway car.

!

For others, they should have known that it wasn't going to be their day. During a robbery in Goodmayes, in Essex, in 1980, a raider who tried to frighten a newsagent by slamming an iron bar on the counter accidentally hit the till and jammed it shut. After unsuccessfully wrestling to open the till, he fled in panic.

!

A gunman who tried to hold up an Ohio bank in January 1983 fled empty-handed after his animated instructions to customers to freeze were followed by the sight of the barrel of his revolver falling off and rolling across the floor. After scrabbling to retrieve it, he could not work out how to replace it. He mumbled 'forget it' and ran off.

!

A sixteen-year-old bank robber in Southend raided a bank close to his home because he said his mother had forbidden him to go too far on his own. Shoppers spotted the suspicious character emerging from the bank in November 1986 still wearing a balaclava mask and holding a replica gun. He was rugby-tackled by a WPC. He later confessed to having got the idea from watching reconstructions on BBC's *Crimewatch*.

!

A man rushed into a Scarborough chemist shop in January 1988 brandishing a gun. He handed the assistant a bag and demanded that it be filled with acne cream. When it was, he grabbed it and escaped.

!

Gerald Rodgers' attempt to rob a local bank in Aberdeen, Missouri, in November 1986 earned him the unenviable title of the world's worst bank robber. His note demanding $3,000 was written on the back of one of his mother's cheques. Although he had tried to delete his mother's name and address, he forgot to do the same to the account number. Police were waiting at his home by the time he returned.

!

Two masked gunmen who tried to rob an old people's home in Peckham, south London, in December 1982 encountered an unexpected difficulty. Their instructions for the residents to lie on the floor were completely ignored – their hearing aids were all tuned to Radio 2. The would-be robbers fled empty-handed.

!

A pensioner in Kiama, New South Wales, held up the local CBC bank in October 1980 wielding a knife and a fork. Harry Fitchett thumped the counter and demanded the bank's money. He was told to leave and did so. He was later arrested in a nearby pub as he ate his dinner.

!

Armed police surrounded a house in Bristol in June 1986 believing that two bank robbers had holed themselves up inside. After a six-hour siege, they stormed the building to find it empty.

!

Coolness under pressure is a prerequisite for the successful heist. Three London jewellery robbers were interrupted in their getaway in November 1981 by a traffic warden who booked them for illegal parking. They calmly waited for her to write out the ticket before speeding off. The car was later found abandoned half a mile away.

!

Thieves broke into a flat in Slough in February 1985 and stole the Alsatian guard dog.

!

The police naturally respond to crime by applying to the full their finely honed investigative skills, as an Essex local paper reported in 1974. In a piece recording the theft of nine 14 ft steel girders from a demolition site in Colchester, it reported that 'the police believe a lorry was used in the theft'.

!

Some characters seem determined to enter the criminal annals and find some curious ways of trying. A Birkenhead youth, who in 1974 threw a brick through a shop window causing £64 worth of damage, returned a week later to ask the manager for his brick back. When he was refused, he complained to the police, who promptly arrested him.

!

A one-legged Bristol man stole a bicycle to get home one night in 1977 and promptly fell off. Police arrested him in hospital.

!

Given the opportunity, criminals will turn any situation to their advantage. In 1981, the changing fortunes of Middle East peace negotiations provided an unlikely arena for sharp pursuits. In October, Israeli police uncovered a sophisticated smuggling ring who understandably couldn't wait for the handover of Israeli-occupied Sinai to Egypt due the following spring. Throughout 1981, a rash of unsolved car thefts in Tel Aviv had baffled police, until an informer led them to discover a vast burial plot in the Sinai desert. In a spirit of cross-border cooperation which might, in other circumstances, have impressed the politicians, it seemed that Israeli and Egyptian gangsters had developed a very cosy relationship. Over 200 deluxe models – Mercedes, Volvos and Peugeots – which sold on the black market in Cairo for ten times their value in Israel, were coated in heavy grease, wrapped in plastic and literally planted in the desert. They would be 'harvested' by Egyptian conspirators in April after the border had moved and the land became Egyptian, thus avoiding the hazardous task of negotiating the strictly guarded frontier. Israeli police could find no precedent for the ruse. Apart from the obvious offence of stealing the vehicles, there appeared to be nothing illegal about the plan as no borders had been crossed and hence no customs laws could be invoked.

!

In May 1977, a Yorkshireman, dubbed as Britain's most optimistic burglar, was advised by magistrates to take up a more rewarding occupation after receiving his seventh conviction. His lack of success might have had something to do with having a withered hand, an artificial leg and only one eye.

!

In January 1982 the Malaysian government uncovered a gruesome fraud involving its civil servants' pension fund. Relatives of those claimants who had died chopped off the thumbs of the departed before burial and used the embalmed digits to continue to provide the thumb prints necessary for encashment of their pension cheques. The scheme was uncovered when the rules were changed to require claimants to collect their money in person. 'Suddenly almost 600 pensioners fell victim to an apparent epidemic and disappeared,' a Government spokesman said.

!

In March 1982 an Italian court sentenced twenty-eight Red Brigade terrorists to jail terms after they were captured and labelled the most inefficient urban terror cell. Their first hold-up to finance their activities netted £6. They were so scared of the one bomb they bought that a 'real terrorist' told them all to give up as they were a danger to everyone. None of the twenty-eight had a driving licence, so they travelled everywhere by bus.

!

The wish of thirty-one-year-old William Cohn, from Miami, to be an air steward seemed doomed when he failed to complete the training programme with Pan Am in 1980. He retained his uniform however and found no difficulty in getting waved through airport security and on to an aircraft without any questions being asked. Once aboard, he would tell the crew that he was travelling on company business and usually offered to help out during the flight. He successfully sustained the charade for two years. His binge of free trips took him all over the world. His downfall came, ironically, because he was simply too good at his job. Passengers were so impressed with his efficiency and courtesy that they wrote to Pan Am in commendation. When the airline tried to find his personnel file to put the letters on, it discovered he didn't have one. He was soon arrested and later charged with theft of flights.

!

When the Boston, Massachusetts, fire department was threatened with manpower cuts in late 1981, two of the firemen hit on the only way to preserve their jobs. In collusion with two police officers whose department also faced economies, they started 163 fires around the city between February 1982 and April 1983. At first the fires were in refuse bins, largely to frighten residents. When that failed to elicit sufficient publicity, they turned to commercial buildings and residential properties, and even included the Massachusetts Fire Academy. When arson indictments were laid in July 1984, the state prosecutor called them the largest the state had ever witnessed.

!

Even Soviet soldiers are not immune to a little dodgy dealing, according to reports reaching the West in August 1985. During manouevres in Czechoslovakia, a tank crew which realised that it had become lost stopped in a village where the only inn was still open. They parked their tank, disembarked and began drinking. Three hours later the soldiers had consumed three bottles of vodka, and had sold the tank to the innkeeper for a further case. The men were found asleep in the forest two days later but couldn't remember what had happened to the tank. Suspicions were aroused two weeks later when the head of a metal recycling plant reported to the authorities an unusual amount of high grade steel he was being offered by a local innkeeper. Investigators found the skeleton of the tank in a shed at the inn. The fate of the innkeeper, and the soldiers, is unrecorded.

!

American's Health and Human Services Secretary, Richard Schweicker, announced in January 1981 the discovery of a loophole in the federal social security regulations which had allowed a Californian man who killed his parents to claim almost $20,000 in benefits for 'orphaned survivors'. The youth found that he was entitled to the money when released on parole and had claimed for five years before any query was raised.

!

The Olympic Games brought an unexpected benefit to Los Angeles in 1984. Officials revealed that one consequence of the massive security operation was that the city enjoyed an entire day free of bank robberies for the first time since October 1979.

!

The Games also produced the most unexpected crime. Less than twenty-four hours after the official close, a bomb was discovered on the coach of the Turkish squad as they were leaving their hotel for the airport. The heroics of a lone LA policeman, who spotted the device and ran with it away from the crowded bus, defusing it moments before it was due to explode, received headlines worldwide. The city's police chief hailed officer James Pearson's bravery.'He showed true courage and had no thought whatsoever for his personal safety. He is a true hero and we are all proud of him.' Unbeknownst to him, Officer Pearson had had more than a little concern for his own personal wellbeing. The following day, the police chief was back in front of the Press to reveal that Pearson had been arrested after confessing to having planted the 'bomb' himself. 'After all the effort the city police force had put into the Games, he was crazy for some individual recognition,' he explained.

!

A fourteen stone Californian woman was acquitted by a San Jose court in March 1983 of killing her son. She had sat on him for two hours as a punishment.

!

Twenty-four-year-old James Riva was sentenced to life imprisonment in Brockton, Massachusetts, in November 1981 for the murder of his grandmother. A self-proclaimed vampire, Riva shot the seventy-four-year-old woman with bullets tipped with gold paint. He testified, 'I've been a vampire for four years. Voices told me to drink blood.' He complained that he had been unable to drink his grandmother's blood because 'she was old and dried up'.

!

A Danish court sentenced Italian Luigi Longhi to indefinite psychiatric confinement in March 1983 for strangling a female hitchhiker. The court was told that before murdering the girl, Longhi had tied her up and washed her hair four times. Since his obsession started at the age of ten, the accused had abducted several women who reported that he had acted without violence or sexual threat and wished only to wash their hair. He confessed to having become frustrated when he ran out of shampoo on the first wash. He then used honey, cottage cheese and vegetable dressing before strangling the twenty-one-year-old West German tourist. He lived for more than nine months with the decomposing body before he was caught.

!

A couple in Maine, USA, were charged in October 1984 of murdering their four-year-old daughter by burning her to death in the family oven. Police were alerted by neighbours who reported hearing cries of 'Let me out, let me out,' and smelling burning flesh. No motive was apparent.

!

At the other end of the scale from murder, so-called 'petty' crime can also however reach astounding proportions:

Earleen Davis, of Houston, Texas, described variously as 'plump' and 'rather large', used her size to perpetrate a series of audacious shoplifting thefts between 1978 and 1981. Holding merchandise between her legs, she wobbled ungainly, but without causing suspicion. She concentrated on fur coats but was caught when she attempted to smuggle out a 20 in colour TV set.

!

People from all walks of life can be tempted. Jack Hanbery was arrested in September 1981 in Atlanta, Georgia, for shoplifting. When questioned by police he gave his occupation: head of the federal penitentiary.

!

Police reported in March 1982 that thefts at Heathrow Airport had fallen sharply since baggage handlers went on strike a fortnight earlier.

!

A shoplifter confessed in an anonymous letter to a Hull chemist shop proprietor, Tim Burrows, in April 1983, that he had stolen a bottle of perfume from the store, but it had borne on his conscience and he wished to make amends. He enclosed a £1 note. The offence had been committed in 1940.

!

Others are less remorseful. Their descent into crime can begin even before they can spell 'remorse'. Police in Hamburg announced in June 1981 that they had broken up the biggest small-time gang that had ever operated in the city. It comprised 307 members, all children. The average age of the gang was thirteen and was responsible for the thefts of 167 cars and 245 cycles and motorcycles. Other charges ranged from arson and possession of deadly weapons to blackmail.

!

In January 1982, Paris police arrested 'Max the Kid', an alleged gang leader and drug addict responsible for over 150 violent muggings on the Metro. He was ten years old.

!

A Miami boy aged five placed prosecutors in a quandary in March 1986 when he confessed to killing his three-year-old playmate. He pushed him off a balcony five storeys up when the toddler had said he wanted to die.

!

At times the motivation for a crime can be the biggest mystery of all. In July 1981, a masked man broke into the Graham household in Virginia Beach, Virginia. All the members of the family were asleep in front of the television. The intruder smeared chocolate and vanilla icing over the twenty-one-year-old wife and left after penning a note: 'See what happens when you leave your doors unlocked'.

!

The village traffic lights at Combwich, Somerset, valued at £2,000, were stolen in May 1982.

!

Police in South Burlington, Vermont, launched a manhunt in June 1986 for a gunman who kidnapped a life-sized statue of a man from outside a restaurant, shot it in the head and dumped it naked in nearby woods. They were unable to suggest a motive.

!

A Bethnal Green man was convicted at London's Bow Street magistrates court in October 1985 for the theft of two crime prevention posters from a hoarding in Leicester Square.

!

A twenty-six-year-old woman in Canon City, Colorado, was prosecuted early in 1982 – for breaking into the local jail to visit her boyfriend in his cell.

!

Nowhere is the perversity of life better illustrated than when art outimitates nature. When police sergeant Osborne of the Surrey constabulary re-enacted the movements of a suspected rapist as part of an investigation in Sutton in February 1981, he got more than he bargained for. Chosen for his similar build and looks, he was 'recognised' and accosted by four zealous dustmen who had seen the photo-fit pictures given wide publicity in the area. Their vigorous attempts at a citizen's arrest landed him in hospital. In the space of ten minutes, police received sixteen other calls from people reporting a sighting of the rapist.

!

In 1985, the American NBC network spent $1.5m on each episode of the hit crime show *Miami Vice*. Miami's real vice squad had a budget of $1.16m to fight crime for the whole of the year.

!

# SEVEN

# WAY OUT WAY OUTS

'*Die, my dear doctor? That is the last thing I shall do.*'
Lord Palmerston, last words, 1865

'*For sale: second hand tombstone. Bargain for family named Perkin.*'

Notice, Nottingham, 1980

!

Death can be unexpected, unintentional, deserved or undeserved, planned or botched. What is certain is that even on the way out, more is said about life than one might think:

The story is told, apocryphal no doubt, of the disc jockey working on a small and remote radio station in Scotland, midway through his programme late at night on 14 October 1977. News came to the station that Bing Crosby had died (the station producer happened to be on the phone to the States and picked the word up almost as it occurred). The DJ thought he could possibly be the first person in the UK to publicly announce the death, so he put on a long track and rushed off to the record library to get an old recording to play. Upon returning, nervously excited by now, he flung the first record onto the turntable without looking and broke into the record then playing with a sombre voice: 'I am deeply sorry to have to inform you listeners that I have just received news from America of a great tragedy. The legendary Bing Crosby is dead. As a humble tribute, I would like to play one of his songs,' and as he switched over to his Crosby 'selection', the melody was beamed out, 'Heaven … I'm in Heaven …'

!

An eighteen-stone man trying to hang himself from an aqueduct over the river Ouse in Buckinghamshire in February 1986 apparently drowned when the rope broke.

!

Dr Wang Cheung, a Chinese doctor living in London, climbed to the roof of the Chinese embassy in December 1981 in order to commit suicide. Having got there, he changed his mind and started to make his way back down, but slipped and fell 40 ft to his death.

!

Louis Frank, of Walthamstow, east London, attempted to commit suicide in March 1981. He planned to take a drug overdose and lie in a bath of hot water. The strain of climbing into the bath caused him to have a heart attack which killed him.

!

Dempr Cevik, a Turkish villager, won an £8 bet in 1974 by eating a whole barbecued lamb. Ten minutes later he dropped dead.

!

A young man died when he dived off a Weymouth jetty in September 1982. The tide was out.

!

William Steyn, an eighteen-year-old Afrikaner soldier, fell victim in 1981 to the system he had elected to devote his life to fighting for. On home leave after a tour of duty with the South African army which had taken him into the tropical bush of Angola, he was involved in a traffic accident near Johannesburg. The ambulance crew sent to his aid took one look at his heavily sun-tanned appearance and thought he was coloured. They leisurely hauled him off to a hospital for non-whites several miles away. The mistake was only discovered when police visited Steyn's family to inform them that their car had been stolen by a coloured youth. His mother recognised the description given as being of her son. Police rushed to transfer him to a hospital for whites but he died before he could be removed.

!

A nineteen-year-old Nottingham man was so afraid of dying that he frightened himself to death, a coroner decided in October 1983. Stephen Smith dreamed of waking up in a coffin and was obsessed with death.

!

Paraskevi Kanima, a sixty-four-year-old Greek woman, died in Athens in September 1983 of what doctors termed 'excessive joy'. A family reunion after sixteen years separation brought on a fatal heart attack as she re-entered her parents' house.

!

An Indonesian MP who had just succeeded in getting a new hearse for his local hospital became its first passenger in January 1986 when he was killed in a road accident on his way home.

!

Sinisa Micic celebrated when he won £40,000 on a local lottery in Yugoslavia in 1986. He went to a bar near Belgrade and bought everyone a drink. He was run over and killed by a lorry as he left.

!

Bella Miller of Torquay died on the morning of her hundredth birthday in July 1986 after opening her message from the Queen.

!

Early in 1974, a sixty-year-old woman awoke to find a dead man jammed in the back window of her home in Herne Hill, south London. Police concluded that he was probably a burglar who died of a heart attack.

!

Norik Hakpioan, a student, died after being caught in a flash fire in his Kensington bedroom in October 1982. He suffered 90 per cent burns in the incident. His brother, who was with him at the time, told the coroner that Norik had been attempting to relieve his piles by using an old family remedy involving paraffin. Police suspected that he had used petrol by mistake and fumes from the open bottle were ignited by a cooker hotplate. The coroner commented that it was the most lethal treatment he had come across in his years as a doctor. A verdict of misadventure was returned.

!

If it's gonna happen, it's gonna happen. The mayor of a Philippine town accidentally shot himself in February 1985 when he slammed his car door on the cocked pistol tucked in his belt. A colleague went to his aid and drove him off to hospital but he died when the car ran out of petrol.

!

Murray Fensome of Luton died in October 1983 from drinking too much. A common fate, one might think. But Murray died from drinking too much water, owing to his obsessive fear that all food and medicine were poison to his body. He would cleanse himself completely by downing excessive quantities of water. After a session in which he drank thirty-five pints he was admitted to hospital unconscious, and later died of water on the brain and water intoxication.

!

In January 1985, police found the body of a young woman in an unclaimed suitcase at Los Angeles international airport. They assumed she must have been a stowaway who had died of hypothermia or asphyxiation.

!

Sixty-two-year-old Iris Somerville was killed in June 1982 while walking through Queens Park in Willesden, north London, when lightning struck the metal support in her bra.

!

John Lacey of Savannah, Georgia, suffered 95 per cent burns in an accident in May 1982. Over forty hospitals refused to admit him though, mainly because he did not possess medical insurance. He died two days later.

!

An eighteen-year-old woman was arrested in Chicago in October 1981 for shooting herself in the stomach to end a six-month pregnancy. The female foetus died of a shotgun wound.

!

Orvell Wyatt Lloyd of Dallas, Texas, told police that he mistook his mother-in-law for a large racoon when he hacked her to death in her garage in 1981.

!

A thirty-one-year-old mother was arrested in Niagara Falls, Ontario, in December 1981 for tying up her two young children, Michelle aged seven and Tyronne aged nine, and scalding them with boiling water to try to drive the devil out of them. Their bodies were found by police in their bedrooms.

!

Crystal Parrington died as a result of being mothered to death. The twenty-eight-year-old woman had never been out of her parents' house in Ramsgate since she had been born because her mother feared she might contract disease. She never went to school and spent most of her life wrapped in sheets, also to protect her from infection, sitting in an armchair. She eventually died, in March 1985, of malnutrition and her grossly deformed body was only 40 ins tall. She weighed only 3 st 7 lb.

!

Two retarded brothers, Louis Hoch, aged thirty-eight and Henry, forty-five, who were incapable of feeding themselves starved to death when their elderly mother died. Police found all three bodies in the family apartment in Queens, New York, in March 1982. Seventy-year-old Mrs Hoch had been dead for about a month. Her sons died shortly afterwards.

!

Joseph Heer, an eighty-nine-year-old recluse, ordered the heating to be cut off to his home in Washington, Pennsylvania, in the middle of January 1986. Police later found him frozen to death in bed along with a box stuffed with $200,000 in cash.

!

Mrs Pang Ok-Ryo, a fifty-three-year-old South Korean, died of apparent exhaustion while carrying out extended prayers for her son's success in a university entrance test. She entered a prayer centre in Uijongbu, near Seoul, on 15 November 1981 and ate nothing until she died ten days later. The result of her son's test is not recorded.

!

A prison protest in Belo Horizonte, Brazil, took a macabre twist in May 1985 when prisoners held a lottery between themselves to see which two would be killed by the inmates to protest at the over owded conditions. The unlucky pair were punched and kicked to death.

!

Inn Siang Ooi, a Miami University student on a field trip in the Costa Rican jungle in August 1986, was stung to death by a swarm of killer bees. In a ferocious attack which eyewitness colleagues compared to a scene from a horror movie, he suffered forty-six stings per square inch of his body.

!

In the southern Indian state of Andhra Pradesh, sixteen passengers died and thirty-seven were injured in May 1986 when their lorry overturned. It had swerved to avoid a man asleep in the middle of the road.

!

Death can be a long time coming. A twenty-five-year-old Bristol woman died in hospital in October 1983 after being in a coma for thirteen years following a road accident. A Yugoslav woman spent twenty-five years in a coma in Zagreb after receiving anaesthetic for an operation, before dying in April 1986. On 11 September 1982, Paul Balay, forty-seven, died after being in a coma for twenty-seven years following a road accident in Lons-le-Saunier, France. However, the longest in recent years is the case of the Venezuelan woman who died in Caracas in December 1985 after lying in a coma for twenty-nine years following a tonsils operation which went wrong.

!

A sprawling tenement block in Tokyo was nicknamed 'Suicide Heights' early in 1981 because of the frequency with which locals decided to end it all from the roof. Within a month of the new year, five people jumped to their deaths, making eighty-four in all since the block was built five years before. The latest, a forty-three-year-old office worker, even left a note apologising to the tenants for the inconvenience he was causing. The apartment block now has nets over the footpath, not to try to save those who jump but to prevent people walking underneath being hit by falling bodies.

!

William Murphy, a Los Angeles drug addict with a history of mental illness, died in September 1982 after digging a hole in his garden and burying himself alive. His mother told police that he had had delusions that he was a mole.

!

A sixty-one-year-old unemployed Nottinghamshire labourer committed suicide in May 1987 by hammering two 5 inch nails into his head. The coroner said he believed it was the first recorded case of this method of suicide.

!

A verdict of death by self-neglect was passed on a fifty-three-year-old north London woman who died in December 1983 weighing only three stone. Jennifer Taylor ate an average of an orange, a biscuit and half a slice of bread a day. In April 1984, a verdict of natural causes was recorded in the case of Catherine Dunbar, a twenty-two-year-old secretary who starved herself to death by obsessive slimming. She weighed only 3 st 4 lb.

!

Antonio Diaz del Rio, forty-one, and his brother, Jose Luiz, thirty-seven, locked themselves in their Madrid flat in August 1982 and starved themselves to death. When police broke into the flat after neighbours had complained about the smell, they found a written record of the previous month entitled 'Diary of a Fast'.

!

At the other end of the scales, so to speak, it took teams of firemen and police to remove the body of Peter Yarnell from his third floor London flat in April 1984. He weighed an estimated 59 stone, and had been confined to the flat for the last two years because he was too large to get through the door. Firemen had to remove the bedroom window and construct a special wooden platform to get his body out. He had troubled the fire brigade before – when in hospital some years previously (and a mere 53 stone), he fell out of bed. It took six firemen to get him back into it.

!

Luis Maria Ortega, a Venezuelan peasant, served a twenty-year sentence for the murder in January 1949 of a cane worker colleague. At his trial, witnesses testified that Ortega had threatened the victim after a fight the day before, and on this circumstantial evidence he was convicted. On his release in 1969, Ortega set about his revenge. He murdered all fifty-six witnesses who had testified against him one by one over a period of thirteen years. He was arrested in February 1982 facing another possible 1,120 years in jail.

!

Helena Burger, whose job it was to warn the other villagers in Illgau, Switzerland, of approaching danger by ringing the church bells, did so at the approach of a thunderstorm in July 1985 just before she was struck by lightning and killed.

!

Woo Bun Kon, a South Korean policeman, got drunk after a quarrel with his wife in April 1982, took his rifle and went on a shooting spree. By the end of the night, he had shot and killed at least seventy-two people in villages around the southern town of Uiryong. He eventually blew himself (and three passers-by) up when he detonated grenades he had stolen during his tour of the neighbourhood. A police spokesman later said that Woo was prone to violence after drinking.

!

Other deaths seem equally to require a little more explanation. The prime example must be Jim Fixx, the American pioneer of the health through jogging craze, who collapsed and died near his home in Vermont on 22 July 1984 – from a heart attack while out jogging.

!

In January 1982, the Vatican reported that a Spanish priest, Father Jose Antonio Moyordomo who worked in a small village in central Spain, had died on 13 November after offering his life to God for the recovery of Pope John Paul II following the assassination attempt on the Pontiff the previous May. Father Moyordomo made his offer in prayers shortly after the shooting. A few days later, he fell ill, and died on the six month anniversary of the event.

!

The cause of Guadelupe Delsma's death in Dallas in February 1983 was a bullet wound – inflicted twenty-two years earlier. Referring to the earlier incident, the coroner said, 'Even though they patched him up and he seemed to suffer no ill effects afterwards, it's still murder, even after twenty-two years'. The local police chief however said that it was most unlikely that the gunman who was convicted of wounding Delsma would be tried for his murder. Locating him after all this time would probably be impossible anyway, he thought.

!

A seventy-eight-year-old woman lay dead in her flat in Westminster for fifteen months, it was reported in October 1985. Her mummified corpse was discovered by gas men who broke in after the bill had not been paid.

!

When police broke into a flat in East Dulwich in July 1986, they discovered the skeletal remains of sixty-year-old Joseph Jamilly tucked up in bed. A pathologist who examined the body estimated that it had lain undisturbed for almost five years. A foot-high pile of mail dating back to December 1981 was found in the hallway, including unpaid bills and final demands. The coroner commented, 'It is extraordinary that such a thing can happen in a civilized city like London. Despite the bills and rates, nobody seemed to be bothered.'

!

An engineer died at Delhi airport in February 1982 after being sucked into the engine of a Boeing 737. The official cause of death was reported as 'shock'.

!

At a funeral in Blairsville, Georgia, in July 1982 to bury Mrs Martha Metcalf, the preacher had just concluded the service by comforting relatives with the words, 'We never know what is going to happen next', when a bolt of lightning struck and killed grandson Donald. Three other members of the family suffered burns.

!

William Hui of Boston, Massachusetts, was shot dead as he sat in his parked car in a busy city street in January 1983. His body lay slumped over the steering wheel for six and a half hours until a passer-by became suspicious and called the police. In that time, two parking wardens had left tickets on the car.

!

The *Voice of Indonesia* newspaper office in Malang received in 1983 through the post a severed human head with fresh blood. Neither the motive nor the identity of the victim was ever discovered.

!

*The Times* had to apologise to the sports commentator Rex Alston in October 1985 when it inadvertently printed his death notice and obituary. Two days later, it announced that Mr Alston was in good health and regretted the distress to his family.

!

There are other bizarre examples, in 'real life', of some pretty close approaches to death's door:

Six hours after he was declared dead, in July 1983, Antonio Franken, a South African road accident victim, was found to be alive and breathing as he was being wheeled into a Cape Town surgery to have his kidneys removed.

!

Jacqueline Rosser was found at her home in Stroud in March 1981 suffering from an apparent drugs overdose. She was rushed to hospital but on arrival she was certified dead and was placed in a coffin in the mortuary. The next day technicians detected signs of life and sent for a resuscitation team which promptly revived her. A report of the incident said that the doctor concerned was not immediately available for comment.

!

A Yugoslav boy survived falling from the seventh floor of a block of flats in Belgrade in December 1985 – by landing on a passing woman, who was unfortunately killed.

!

An unidentified seventeen-year-old construction worker fell 50 ft from the top of the building on which he was working in September 1984. He suffered only a broken nose. When he saw the blood, he promptly fainted.

!

Apostolos Poulios, who took two sleeping pills to help him sleep in September 1984, slept so soundly that after twenty hours his wife called the undertakers. They were beginning to give him his last shave before burial when he woke up.

!

Otto Henning attempted suicide while on holiday in Manhattan in November 1987. Jumping from the four-teenth floor of the President Hotel, he landed on a terrace two floors below. He jumped again and reached only a tenth floor extension. He gave up when he realised he had broken his arm in the process.

!

A Brisbane man tried to decapitate himself with a circular saw after a row with his girlfriend. The police report in June 1982 said that the unidentified man had been thrown out of the flat in which he lived with the woman. He went to where he worked, grabbed the saw and placed it against his neck. He then switched it on, inflicting a deep wound to his throat. He calmly drove back to the flat to show the girl. Her screams alerted a neighbour who called the police. Doctors agreed that he was lucky to be alive. 'The bone was showing, but he narrowly missed several major blood vessels', one said. The man was admitted for psychiatric treatment.

!

A New Zealand priest suggested in 1981 that people would benefit emotionally by digging the graves for their own dead. Writing in his Auckland parish magazine, Rev Eugene O'Sullivan believed that 'working in close proximity to the departed and to their fellow bereaved could serve to share grief ... and save $50 on the mechanical excavator'.

!

A Californian company announced in February 1981 the latest aid for the bereaved – the talking tombstone. For $10,000 ('but sure to come down in price if there is mass demand') a solar-powered tape recorder with twin speakers could be inserted into your loved one's gravestone. It would have capacity to play a ninety-minute recording. Those wishing to leave a permanent record would record their message before the big day to be replayed each time relatives visited the grave. Stanley Zelazny, who patented the idea and took five years to develop the system, was confident there was a market. 'Instead of coming to look at a slab of stone, relations will be able to hear their departed's voice talking to them. It would be a so much more fulfilling experience.'

!

In 1982, at the height of martial law in Poland, the town council of Kazimierz Wielki announced that because of restrictions in supply the only people permitted to buy new suits would be dead ones, 'so that the body may be respectable in its coffin'. Shoes or boots could be procured 'only under very special circumstances'.

!

The authorities in Genoa, Italy, announced plans in June 1986 to relieve the chronic shortage of burial plots in the city, which had only 35 cemeteries for its 750,000 citizens. They produced a design for a 130 ft, 10 storey glass skyscraper, which would hold 10,000 bodies and also offer pleasant views of the mountains and the sea. The plan was scotched after civil aviation managers reported that it would lie in the flight path of aircraft using the city airport. There were enough unburied bodies as it was, they felt, without inviting more.

!

The wish to be remembered takes on curious forms. When Andre Tchaikowsky, a Polish exile living in Oxford, died in August 1982, he bequeathed his skull to the Royal Shakespeare Company for use in productions of Hamlet. Executors of the estate delivered the skull in a box to startled staff at the RSC after the will's reading in which he recalled his childhood ambitions for a career on the stage.

!

An inquest in January 1985 heard that a daughter, devoted to her ninety-year-old mother, kept her body for a year after the woman died. She fed her liquids every day and talked to the body in the bedroom. On her birthday she was given brandy. A police report said that the body had begun to mummify.

!

'We will remember them.' Well, not always. Amongst items reported lost on Japanese National Railways in 1975 were nine urns, complete with human ashes.

!

Tom Gribble of Bristol announced in June 1983 that his will stipulated that his body should be cremated and his ashes used for an egg-timer and handed down to future generations. 'It is my way of being of use to my family,' he said.

!

In January 1988, police in Knoxville, Illinois, discovered the mummified body of a man who had been dead for eight years being nursed and cared for by his wife and two children who were apparently unaware that he was dead. Having regularly been dressed, spoken to and dragged around the house, the body of Carl Stevens had been reduced to bones. A police investigator said that the family appeared to have 'abnormal beliefs in the power of healing'.

!

A newspaper in Indonesia reported in February 1986 that a thirty-four-year-old man had remained standing on his front doorstep for fourteen years as a self-inflicted punishment for ill-treating his mother who had died.

!

William Cox, of Littleport, in Cambridgeshire, kept his mother's body at home for thirteen years after she had died in 1972. For the first seven years he kept the body walled up in a bedroom, then he put it in a home-made coffin and wheeled it on a bicycle through the town to his own home where he put it in a shed. It was only when the DHSS began to make enquiries about his mother, whose pension he continued to draw despite having over £400,000 savings himself, that he buried the body in the garden. Police dug it up in March 1985.

!

John Wilson was certainly remembered by the people who knew him. In the mid-term Congressional elections in November 1982, electors in Austin, Texas, re-elected him as state senator, even though he had died forty-four days before the poll.

!

When Ernest Digweed, a Portsmouth recluse, died in 1977 he stipulated in his will that proceeds from his investments, worth about £350,000, should go to Jesus Christ if he reappeared on Earth before the year 2000. He would have to prove his identity (it was not stated how) in order to claim the money. (It was subsequently reported in 1981 that two claimants had already tried but failed.) The Public Trustees Office decided in the meantime to award the estate to two distant cousins with the advice that they should seek appropriate insurance coverage just in case the will had to be honoured.

!

In January 1987 the Liberal peer, Lord Avebury, announced his intention to include in his will the provision that his body be fed to stray dogs at Battersea Dogs Home. 'I believe that anything that is biodegradable should be recycled,' he said. The Home's manager voiced diplomatic reservations about the ethics of the request, although he admitted that he was sure there was much nutritional value in the noble Lord.

!

At the end of the day, so to speak, there will always be those who manage to exploit death to their own benefit:

Staff in the intensive care ward of a hospital in Las Vegas, gambling capital of the world, were suspended in March 1980 for organising a sweep stake on estimating how long critically ill patients would live. Police were called to investigate after officials suspected that some patients had had their oxygen supplies tampered with, presumably in an attempt to influence the outcome of the wagers. Up to six deaths were reported to be suspicious and under investigation.

!

Only slightly less tasteless was the report in 1981 that an Ohio research group, commissioned by the US government to look into ways of improving pedestrian safety, had requested, and got, human corpses for use in experiments. They were positioned in key places and struck by cars. The institute said they were 'much more life-like' than dummies.

!

Finally, it wasn't long before the video was brought to bear on death. In December 1981, an Australian company announced 'Video Wills', a service which, for $100, provided clients with a recording of their last will and testament, to be played after their death to their assembled family. Designed to 'leave a permanent memory in "living" colour', it proved also an opportunity for some forthright language from the safe haven of the grave. A sensitive editing policy had to be adopted and clients soothed if emotion got the better of them. One woman who decided she was not after all going to leave anything to someone who had always thought he would get most of her estate, promptly and explicitly told him the reasons for her decision. Another spent most of the time doling out her many cats to unwilling relations with conditions attached to each. Mostly, however, the service was reported to be favourably used. 'They're real touching,' said one company officer.

!

# EIGHT

# **TROUBLE AND STRIFE**

'*Years ago I had money to burn and my wife was the perfect match.*

Busker's card, Kensington, 1979

'*Insanity is hereditary. You get it from your kids.*'

Graffiti, London, 1979

!

Indonesian Ali Nasution, twenty-eight, was jailed for seven years by a Sumatran court in February 1981 for polygamy. He had married 121 women since 1974. His plea for mitigation rested on the fact that he had already divorced 93 of them.

!

Udaynath Dakhinray, an Indian landowner from Orissa, married his eighty-ninth bride in August 1985. Of his previous 88, 57 had left or divorced him and 26 had died. Dakhinray had pledged himself to a life of polygamy after his first wife had left him 36 years before, after just two weeks.

!

A fourteen-year-old Kenyan girl called Suldano married 'the man of my dreams' in Nairobi in November 1984: one hundred-year-old Muhammed Aloo. 'Older men really know how to treat a girl,' she said. 'He is always kind and never beats me.'

!

Luther Mansfield, from Louisville, Kentucky, married the lady of his dreams in March 1983, but after six months he and his wife, Annie, decided that life together was too dangerous. Luther had just given her an almost fatal overdose of drugs after misreading the label on the jar. 'We are too old to look after each other,' he said. He was 95; she was 101.

!

Soviet newsagency TASS reported in August 1983 that Niftulla Agayev and his wife Balabeim had celebrated their hundredth wedding anniversary in the village of Lerit, in Azerbaijan. He was 126; she was 116. They were said to have 150 children, grandchildren and great-grandchildren, and were still active on their farm.

!

In August 1979, twenty-year-old South African Susanna van Zul married Silas van Aswegan, sixty-two, the widower of her grandmother. She thus became her mother's stepmother.

!

Chen Yuanfeng, a twenty-six-year-old school teacher from Hubei in central China, refused to marry the man chosen for her by her family in February 1983. Instead, she went ahead and married her own choice in a secret ceremony. When she announced what she had done, her family had her abducted and buried alive.

!

Patricia Smith was jailed by a Harrogate court in October 1982 for her third offence of bigamy in six years. During the same period she had contracted three lawful marriages as well. All had been to soldiers – 'she was fatally fascinated by men in uniform', her defending counsel said – and all ended in disaster.

!

Jail officials in California refused to allow convicted spy Andrew Lee to get married in 1981 because he could not demonstrate a 'compelling reason'. According to the prison rule book, a spokesman said, 'being in love is not good enough'.

!

Police in Rio de Janeiro, called to intervene in a domestic dispute in June 1981, found Rodriguez Valdez trying to push his wife into a sewer. Blaming her constant nagging, he said later that he would have succeeded if she had not become stuck in the manhole on account of her 'gross fatness'.

!

A Glasgow court heard in May 1982 that the strained marriage of William and Doris Gebbie was saved when Doris stabbed her husband with a bread knife during a fight. Thinking that she was being strangled, she had stabbed him in the chest. The knife hit a rib and failed to penetrate. The defence counsel at Doris's subsequent trial for malicious wounding reported that 'these bizarre circumstances in fact have enhanced the couple's relationship and the romance is now blossoming after years of married misery and torment'.

!

Lille housewife Rochelle Vignal became fed up with neighbours parking outside her home. After weeks of vain pleading, she arose before dawn one morning in February 1982 and set to work on the gleaming new Citroën in front of her gate. She exuberantly scratched the paintwork with a wire brush, poured three pints of paint over the roof and slashed the tyres before slinking back to her bed. She was awakened later by her husband who wanted to announce his anniversary present to her ... a new Citroën.

!

A couple with ten children living in a state-owned block of flats in Nantes were ordered in April 1982 to remove the nine-month-old pet lion after complaints from neighbours.

!

Residents of a three-storey building in one of Naples' oldest districts argued with fire and police officers for three hours in February 1982 when the authorities declared the building unsafe and ordered its evacuation. As the argument continued, by agreement, in the street, the block fell down.

!

A new dimension in housing choice was unveiled in May 1981 with the first sales by the Pentagon of obsolete nuclear missile silos as 'dream homes'. Typical of what was on offer, in Wyoming, was the former home of a 100 ton Atlas missile, targetted on Moscow. For an attractive £1,500 (original construction cost – £2m) the lucky couple got 830 square metres of floor space, enough for three bedrooms, two bathrooms, a kitchen and a dining room, and a front door weighing 400 tons. Other selling points, the Pengaton suggested, were good insulation, a burglar-proof environment and, naturally, a very reliable nuclear fallout shelter.

!

No matter what the circumstances, the inexorable rise in the cost of living is cause enough for everyone to complain. It was reported that a West Yorkshire man had complained in the spring of 1981 about the 450 per cent increase in his council rent. His present bill was 58p a week.

!

Local advertisements for sale of household items can reveal more about the vendor's domestic life than they might think, as the following examples show:

White satin and lace wedding dress. 38″ bust. Only worn three times.

Manchester 1979

Cheap. Electric guitar and powerful amplifier. Phone —. If boy answers please ring off and call later.

Basingstoke 1979

Double bed, 6ft 7in × 5ft. Less than one year old. Only half used...

Ulster 1976

German linguaphone course. Unused wedding ring. Offers...

Bucks 1980

Five speed racing bike ... new, just needs putting back together.

Redruth 1980

Very old mantelpiece ... as new.

Warrington 1980

Young scientist's rocket kit for sale, used once only. Also good home wanted for only white mouse in neighbourhood who knows what it looks like from 50 ft up.

San Francisco 1978

Book, *The Art of Investment.* Cost £123, will accept £65.

Leicester 1981

1971 Mini: quantity of spares and summons to prove it did 55 mph on 6 June.

Chelsea 1983

**!**

Out of the mouths ... only children have the remarkable talent to perceive the world in healthy innocence:

Small girl seeing Buckingham Palace for the first time: 'Our front garden is concreted over too'.

Primary maths pupil's answer to question, 'take 9 from 246 as many times as possible': 'I did it fifty times and I always got 237.'

Twelve year old in French class being asked the difference between Madame and Mademoiselle: 'Monsieur'.

Eleven year old's environmental studies essay on the effect of oil pollution: 'When my mum opened a tin of sardines last night it was full of oil and all the sardines were dead.'

Ten year old's response to question, 'When dead, what do you want to be remembered for?': 'Ever.'

Twelve year old's response to the question, 'why does a surgeon wear a mask when he performs an operation?': 'So if he makes a muck of it the patient won't know who did it.'

Ten year old's reply to 'what famous London landmark has a figure with only one eye?': 'Cleopatra's needle.'

Twelve year old's essay on 'what would you do to encourage motorists to show more consideration for others?': 'Drive a police car.'

Seven year old's reply to 'why do we say "Amen" after prayers?': 'It's a special way or saying over and out to God.'

!

Some learn the ways of the world very quickly:

A five-year-old boy seeing a rainbow for the first time said to his mother, 'What advert is that for?'

A seven year old going to his first carol service demanded indignantly when the collection plate came round, 'You mean we have to pay for this?'

An eight year old playing the innkeeper in a nativity play added a temperamental though evidently heartfelt ad lib when Joseph and Mary arrived at his door. He declared to Mary, 'You may enter, but Joseph can — off because he took the part I wanted to play.'

Three 6 year-old kings in a Derby nativity play presented their gifts solemnly. The first said, 'Gold', the second said 'Myrrh', and the third said, 'And Frank sent this.'

A seven year old hearing a rector in his Norfolk church declare that this was the 'Year of Our Lord 1982' asked, 'Is that like last year was the Year of the Disabled 1981?'

!

Throughout Australia on Palm Sunday, churches distribute palm crosses to their congregations. Outside St James church, Sydney, in 1982 two small boys were later seen sword-fighting with theirs.

!

A nine year old became one of America's youngest bank robbers when he held up a Manhattan bank in February 1981. Armed with a silver pistol, which police later said was a replica, he was just tall enough to peer over the counter. He demanded money and ran off with just over $100. Asked to describe him, a cashier said, 'Very cute'.

!

A United Nations family planning team reported in September 1982 their difficulties in getting the message across to remote villagers in Indonesia. After demonstrating with bamboo sticks how to wear condoms, they returned some weeks later to find villagers wearing them on their fingers or adorning their huts with condom-covered poles.

!

Australian health officials abandoned a sex education campaign for aboriginals in 1981 after they found that women believed that singing the jingle which had been composed to make the advice memorable was sufficient protection against pregnancy.

!

More than 700 Thai men marked the fifty-fifth birthday of King Bhumibol in December 1981 by having a vasectomy as part of a mass birth control programme. A team of thirty-six surgeons performed the seven-minute operations under local anaesthetic in a cluster of tents and caravans in the centre of Bangkok.

The following year, on the King's fifty-sixth birthday, the campaign claimed a world record of 1,202 vasectomies in the ten-hour session, a rate of one every two minutes.

!

Robert Crutison from Oklahoma was intent on a home birth for his first child in January 1982. Police reported later that when he discovered that the baby was too big for a normal delivery, he used a razor to perform a caesarian section, sewing up his twenty-six-year-old wife with household needle and cotton. While the baby was said to be doing fine, Mrs Crutison had to undergo emergency surgery in hospital.

!

On 6 March 1983, thirty-year-old Lillian Green from Walsall gave birth to her third son. Her first was born on 6 March 1978 and her second on 6 March 1980.

The Cummins family of Clintwood, Virginia, set an astonishing record with their five children. Ralph and Carolyn's first, Catherine, was born on 20 February 1952. Carol followed on 20 February 1953; Charles on 20 February 1956; Claudine on 20 February 1961 and Cecilia on 20 February 1966.

!

In September 1981, Leontina Alvina, a fifty-five-year-old Chilean housewife, reportedly gave birth to her fifty-first child. During the course of her lifetime's devotion to child rearing, she had produced seven pairs of twins and four sets of triplets. She had remained married to the same man throughout.

!

A father in Jordan was jailed for six months in December 1981 for making his two teenage daughters carry him around Amman in a specially constructed sedan chair.

!

In February 1982 it was reported from India that a father in Andhra Pradesh, who borrowed £40 from a loan shark a year before and was unable to make the repayments, had agreed to give his two daughters in settlement. The money-lender valued the elder at £300 and the younger at £250, enough to cover the interest charges.

!

A French couple were arrested on child abuse charges in August 1982 after twelve-year-old David Brisson was found sleeping in a garden near his house in the Paris suburb of Bretigny-sur-Orge. Illiterate and semi-articulate, he told police that he had been locked in rooms in his home since he was five. For the last year, he had been locked in a closet. He had escaped when his mother forgot to lock the closet before going away for a few days.

!

Australian police announced in July 1982 the discovery of a thirty-seven-year-old mentally retarded man who had been kept by his family for more than twenty years in a bricked-up room on their farm in the Victorian outback. Pest controllers who had been called to the farmstead in the tiny hamlet of Diapur, in the remote Western Districts, found Douglas Smith, who was incapable of speech and living in appalling conditions in the tiny windowless room. After removing him to a hospital, police said that in keeping him on the farm, his parents, both in their eighties, and his two middle-aged sisters, appeared to have acted 'out of misguided loyalty rather than cruelty'.

!

A family of hermit children was discovered by social service officials in the Lancashire fishing port of Fleetwood in December 1982. The four children, two girls and two boys, aged between five and nine, were reported to have hardly ever left the council house in which they had all been born. Neighbours said that they communicated with each other by animal howls and were only seen peering through the curtains of their bedrooms. A health visitor found them pale, inarticulate, frightened of sunlight and not toilet trained. An eight-year-old girl was still in nappies. Their parents denied neglecting them.

!

The *China Daily* reported in August 1981 that a man from Hunan province, who had already fathered a child before becoming a woman in a sex change operation, was about to have a baby him/herself.

!

When Newton Friedman was divorced by his estranged wife, Carol, in May 1986, he entered a request for visiting rights – to play the two baby grand pianos at the family home, for four hours, twice a week.

!

John Bartram took his own revenge in May 1981 after his wife, from whom he had separated, succeeded in obtaining a court injunction forcing him to move out of the family home in Surrey, which he had built himself. Unable to bear to see her derive sole benefit from the proceeds of its sale, he set light to it. The £65,000 bungalow was gutted.

!

Eugene Schneider, of Carteret, New Jersey, lost his divorce suit in 1975 and was ordered by the court to divide his property equally with his wife. The following day he chain-sawed his house in two.

!

Virgil Everhart of Central City, Kentucky, decided in January 1983 to initiate his divorce settlement by sawing his house in two with a chain saw. It took a day to cut through most of the flooring in the single storey house. He even hired an acetylene torch to divide the bathtub. He said he intended to live in his half of the home.

!

A San Francisco author who made millions by writing books on how to succeed by cheating was sued for $2m by his ex-wife after she read his new bestseller. Robert Morrison's petard was hoisted in August 1981 when he wrote *Divorce Dirty Tricks*, an account of how he evaded his liabilities to his wife when they divorced. Describing his tactics as 'legalised thuggery', he introduced the book as a guide to 'how to take someone's hide before they know what's happened to them'. He then enumerated the manouevres he had deployed to persuade his wife that it would be good for her morale and independence if he did not give her the $½m he had originally promised, hide from her most of their communal property by complicated registration practices through his companies to conceal ownership and even get her to return money he had already given her, with interest. The outcome of the wife's suit is not recorded.

Morrison's other successful works included *How to Steal a Job*, *The Greedy Bastard's Business Manual*, and *Why SOBs Succeed and Nice Guys Fail in Small Businesses*.

!

Saowaphark Pruempiti, a seventeen-year-old Bangkok girl was attacked in her house in February 1983 by an admiring intruder. When he tried to steal a kiss, she bit off his tongue. She told police he ran away screaming. Police took away the tongue as evidence.

!

One of the unexpected consequences of the war between Iran and Iraq has been the formidable advance in women's rights in the strictly Islamic regime in Iran. Before, a wife always walked dutifully several paces behind her husband. With the onset of war, and amid the abandoned explosives and unexploded mines, a wife was soon encouraged to stride proudly out in front of him.

!

# NINE

# **A LITTLE LEARNING**

*'If my darling Jessica is in need of strictness, please will you shout at the child next to her. That will be sufficient to upset her.'*

Parent's note to teacher, 1979

*'Diagnostic and Remedial Spelling Manuel with accompanying Teacher's Manuel.'*

Book order from school, Wallingford, Oxon, 1981

**!**

The US Army spent $160m in 1981 on a basic education programme in an effort to raise standards among its troops. Government accounting officers reviewing the programme after a year discovered that only 17 per cent of eligible soldiers had signed up for the lessons, and only 13 per cent of those had managed to pass. An estimated 45 per cent of the enlisted army had reading and mathematical skills below the level normally attained by fifteen year olds...

**!**

...but that doesn't say much. A 1983 survey of Dallas twelve year olds found that more than 20 per cent of them were unable to find the United States on a world map. The Federal Education Secretary was reported to be dismayed by the results which, he said, bore out an earlier study which concluded that America had been committing 'unilateral educational disarmament'. Another study in 1986, of seventeen year olds, revealed that only 32 per cent knew in which half-century the American Civil war took place, a third were unable to find Vietnam on a map and a fifth thought that the Vietnam War had come before the Second World War.

!

A company called the Open University of Washington DC offers a wide range of courses for the less than discerning prospective student. Its 1985 brochure included a course of 'Sex, Sex and More Sex', offering the opportunity to 'learn what men and women really want in bed; turn-ons and turn-offs; driving your partner wild; and mistakes not to make in bed'. Also available were 'Dare To Go Bare' or 'Are You Serious About Your Tan?'; 'How to Pick Up Women', 'How To Pick Up Men' and 'How To Marry Money'.

!

An adult education organisation called 'The Learning Annex', also based in Washington, was offering a similar array of courses by 1987. Described by the director, William Zanker, as 'simply aimed at matching human needs', the courses included 'Flirting', 'Massage for Couples', 'Sexual Secrets of the Orient', and 'Stripping for your Partner'. Other esoteric subjects on offer were dog sledding, dancing the mambo and a shower singers' workshop.

!

Auckland University abandoned an adult education course on 'optimisation and optimal control' in 1982 because nobody turned up for its first lecture, due largely to no-one understanding what it was all about. The explanatory guide described the content as 'the static problem considering conditions for optimality and computational methods for first the unconstrained minimisation of a non-linear function and then function minimisation to fixed constraints'.

!

A Jordanian newspaper reported in January 1985 that a pupil sitting for secondary examinations in Amman was caught cheating by concealing a matchbox-sized radio receiver in his Arab headdress. A friend outside the classroom read him his answers.

!

When Morgan Lamb failed the examinations for the Los Angeles bar, he got his wife to impersonate him for the re-sits. Laura Salant, a former federal prosecutor, tied her hair tightly back and painted on thick eyebrows for the identification photograph required to enter the exam hall. She sailed through, turning Morgan's failure into third place out of almost 7,700 entrants. If that was not enough to cause suspicion, an invigilator had already noticed something odd about 'Mr Lamb'. 'He' was seven months pregnant at the time. She was given three years probation in March 1988 for false personation; he faced four years in jail for fraud.

!

Robert Amparan, a San Diego headmaster, implemented the ultimate scheme to cut truancy rates in his school. In November 1980 he began to pay his children, who came from the mainly poor district of the city, 10c a day to attend. In the first term, absences fell to 7 per cent, half the previous level.

!

Even if you can keep them in class, there is a weight of evidence that the pearls of wisdom imparted by the teachers do not always reach their targets undimmed. The following excerpts from students' writings demonstrate some novel wrong turns on the road to knowledge:

'Martin Luther first came to the historian's eye in 1517 when he nailed his ninety five faeces to the church door at Wittenburg.'

'The Romans built Hadrian's Wall so they could jump over it and surprise the Scots.'

'A sixty-foot tree can break wind for up to 200 yards.'

'A common disease of cereal crops is wheat germ.'

'The light passes into the eye, through the lens and is focused on the rectum.'

'The Royal Wedding was a whore inspiring event.'

'They would be in just the same position as the Liberals had been in in 1886, only worse.'

'Between 1935 and 1964 there were no less than fifty-six successful coups. This averages out at between one and three every year.'

'Vasco de Gama swept across the Atlantic in a wide ark.'

'Photoperiodism occurs in animals when they hibernate and shed their leaves.'

'In Australia, they put mosquito nets over the beds at night to keep out the incest.'

'He spent his days in prison sewing children's balls together.'

'Socrates died from an overdose of wedlock.'

'I don't know what the speed of light is, but it always arrives far too early in the morning.'

!

The catalogue for a large and well-known bookshop in Oxford listed three novels entitled *Nothing*, *Doting*, and *Blindness* written by 'a fine author who has been unaccountably neglected'. The catalogue omitted to give his name.

!

In October 1976 the South African authorities finally permitted the publication of a thriller by Mickey Spillane. It was entitled *The Long Wait*.

!

In September 1982, bookseller Peter Miller mounted, as a joke, a stall at the York Book Fair exhibiting his collection of 'the world's worst literary failures'. It turned out to be a roaring success and hundreds of buyers eagerly sought to acquire volumes such as *The Romance of Leprosy* and *Cooking With God*. A 650-page masterpiece on stopcocks in Liverpool's Liver building went in ten minutes and a book on a *Ramble in Germany* which had lain on the shelf for thirteen years was snapped up within the hour. *Backwards to Lake Como*, the story of an obscure Victorian man who walked backwards from London to Italy, fetched £2. Other titles to go included *The Sex Life of Robinson Crusoe*, a monograph on *The Teasel as a Carnivorous Plant*, and *Heroes and Heroines of Liberia*.

!

The Frankfurt Book Fair of that year also recognised novelty. Among the titles on display were *Braces Owners Manual: A Guide to the Wearing and Care of Braces*; *Social Odours in Mammals*; *Keeping Warm With an Axe*, and *What Do Socks Do?*

!

The Russian Language Institute of the Soviet Academy of Science announced in early 1984 that its latest work was completed and about to be printed: a multi-volume listing of every word used by Lenin in his writings with page and volume references to their exact location in his complete collected works. There are 37,500 words, of which 12,000 occur only once.

!

Professor Sem Dresden received a $100,000 award in November 1985 for a literary work that was not even half finished. His prize, from the Alexander Onassis Public Benefit Foundation, was for the compilation of the complete works of the fifteenth-century religious philosopher, Erasmus. The project was begun in 1969, since when thirteen volumes have appeared; a further seventeen remain to be published, the delay being chiefly due to unseemly squabbles among the august scholars as to who would get the best parts to edit. It is not expected that the magnus opus will be finished until the end of the century at the earliest. Despite his laurels, Professor Dresden confided that the whole thing was an 'idiotic enterprise'.

!

At the height of the financial crisis which eventually led to the takeover of the *Daily Telegraph* in early 1985, the newspaper continued to advertise one of its most popular publications, *101 Ways to Run a Business Profitably*.

!

In April 1980, the English Theatre of Amsterdam claimed a world record for reading the complete works of Shakespeare in thirty hours, beating the previous record held by a Wakefield drama college by almost six hours.

!

The Government announced in the autumn of 1982 that the Ulster Yearbook would henceforth be published biennially.

!

A woman who returned six overdue library books in the Melbourne suburb of Balwyn in 1982 received a computerised bill – for $202,926,013.51.

!

An amnesty at a Bracknell library in 1983 produced over 1,000 overdue books, including three romantic novels borrowed in 1939.

!

Pick of the bunch, however, belongs to the Free Library of Trenton, New Jersey. In September 1985 a volume which had been loaned to Haverford College, Pennsylvania, was finally returned – 188 years late.

!

The use of jargon is perhaps the most obvious way of attempting to demonstrate that one is a little more learned than the rest. It does not, however, always seem to work:

From a sociologist's letter in *New Society*, April 1979: 'Britain has irreversibly become a poly-ethnic as well as a multi-racial society.'

!

From a US aviation weekly, August 1982: 'Boeing's system exhibits cost benefits only beyond the complexity level at which its cost/complexity curve crosses that of a competing system.' (In other words, it's more expensive.)

!

The Australian and New Zealand Association for the Advancement of Science conference in 1982 included a session on 'Organisational Aspects of Communication'. The centrepiece was a paper by a Dr H Irwin, enlighteningly titled 'A Constructivist-based Communication Competence Scale for Face-to-Face Interaction at the Interpersonal-Organisational Interface'. (Or, presumably, 'How to talk to your bosses'.)

!

The *Psychological Record* provided this report of the eye-opening conclusions of an experiment in 1986: 'Three experiments were conducted with pigeons to compare the effects of shifting a multiple variable interval variable interval (mult V1 V1) baseline condition to multiple signaled-variable interval variable interval (mult sig-V1 V1) and multiple extinction variable interval (mult EXT V1). In experiment 1, the mult sig-V1 V1 treatment condition generated more instances of no interaction (ie, no change in response rate in the unaltered V1 component) and negative induction (ie, a decrease in response rate in the unaltered V1 component) than positive contrast ...'

!

From the Seventh Directive on Company Accounting, issued by the European Commission in 1983 to 'clarify' the treatment of consolidated company accounts by EC member countries, comes this illuminating gem: 'For the purposes of Paragraph 1 above, any subsidiary undertaking of a subsidiary undertaking shall be considered a subsidiary undertaking of the parent undertaking which is the parent of the undertaking to be consolidated.'

!

The Analysis of Merchant Shipping Accident Report Forms (October 1982–March 1983) produced by the Department of Transport provided this unfathomable insight into the current definition of a 'dangerous occurrence': 'The Department of Transport is interested in certain types of dangerous occurrence. These types are listed in the Regulations and in Annex 6. If such a dangerous occurrence occurs, it has to be reported on an accident report form whether or not it has caused a reportable accident. The Department treats (as in the figures below) those dangerous occurrences which cause a reportable accident as a reportable accident, and those which did not cause a reportable accident as a dangerous occurrence. Normally dangerous occurrences did not cause a reportable accident and, it would seem, not many caused a non-reportable accident. This is probably because people are more careful in situations which they recognise to be dangerous.'

!

This stentorian piece of verbiage, from a nursing journal in 1985, is succour to every nurse's heart: 'The main goal for nursing is to assist the client towards optimal wellness. A systems model explains how system stability is achieved in relation to the stresses, that is, to retain attain and/or maintain an optimal wellness or stability level. The degree of stability is equated with the degree of wellness, placing wellness and illness on a continuum.'

!

In case you find computers intimidating, help is at hand, through for example these instructions thoughtfully provided by a Leicestershire scientific instruments company: 'The options in the file are processed as though they replace the OPTIONS option. Consequently, the OPTIONS option in one option file can refer to another option file. Options files can be chained together in this manner. Alternatively, the OPTIONS option in the SCRIPT command line might refer to a file that contains a list of OPTIONS options, each of which points to a different options file.'

!

A high street bank recently informed a customer of his refund in the following deliciously personal terms: 'I have input an abatement against any credit-cleared monies which are held in your account.'

!

The Institute of Scientific and Technical Communicators uncovered the following aid to understanding from an aircraft electronics manual: 'The internal guidance system uses deviations to generate corrective commands to fly the aircraft from a position where it is to a position where it isn't. The aircraft arrives at the position where it wasn't, thus, the position where it was is the position where it isn't. In the event that the position where it is now is not the same as the position where it originally wasn't, the system will acquire a variation (variations are caused by external factors and discussion of these factors is beyond the scope of this simple explanation) ...'

!

In April 1981, the US Navy was forced to scrap a multi-million dollar computer system which had been installed in its assault ship *Nassau*. It was a prototype of a revolutionary automatic propulsion control device, but naval command soon discovered that it was too complicated for the sailors to operate, and they could not afford the cost of training the crew. 'We had anticipated a certain level of competence in the crew which simply wasn't there,' a spokesman said. 'It was cheaper to instal a simpler system.'

!

Chinese scientists reported in January 1981 the exploits of two young sisters, Wang Qiang, aged twelve, and Wang Bin, ten, who were said to have the power to read with their ears and armpits. The *Workers Daily* said that experiments had successfully been concluded in which they identified characters placed next to their ears or under their arms. They also possessed a form of X-ray vision, being able to indicate the position of scars on the bodies of fully-clothed witnesses. A girl from Hunan was also reported to be able to read with her buttocks, and able to peel an orange through thought alone.

!

The Soviet newspaper *Isvestia* reported in June 1987 the case of Yuliya Vorobyeva, a thirty-seven-year-old Ukrainian woman who had developed X-ray vision after suffering near electrocution several years earlier. In experiments, she had been able to correctly identify foodstuffs which witnesses had eaten by looking at their stomachs, and was able to make medical diagnoses on hospital patients.

!

Not only people are reported to have strange powers. The Chinese *Shanxi Daily* reported in February 1981 the discovery of a rock in central Hunan province which cries for help. The paper speculated that the rock, which juts out of Dongting lake, could be magnetic and 'recorded sounds of drowning sailors. When conditions of sunlight and temperature are right, it could then play the sounds back again'.

!

Research is the lifeblood of most 'scientists', although it is not always immediately apparent what some projects can gainfully offer to the world. A Swedish university once passed a PhD thesis which showed that elderly people moved faster when they were in a hurry than when they weren't. However, things are not always even as clear cut as that. The pursuit of knowledge has thrown up some curious offerings in recent years:

A major research programme on environmental pollution undertaken by Australian scientists in 1981 concluded that the most serious cause of air pollution on the planet was burping cows. The concentration of methane in the atmosphere was recorded as increasing by 1 per cent a year, mostly due to the doubling of the number of cattle in the previous decade. 'They burp it up; they don't fart it out,' Dr Paul Fraser reported. 'They do a lot of belching ... it could be many litres each burp, up to 300 litres a day.'

!

'Scientific' research by American Dr Joyce Brothers in 1982 revealed that, on average, an American woman kissed seventy-nine times before marriage.

!

Research conducted in 1983 by a reputable British survey company made this major contribution to understanding the habits of British leisure seekers. It claimed to have found a 'direct correlation' between people's leisure activities and the television programmes they watched. Its astonishing findings included the unexpected discovery that anglers were three times more likely to watch 'Go Fishing' than non-fishing men; and 76 per cent of 'Garden Calendar' viewers said they were gardeners.

!

Among the research studies that have won the Wisconsin Senator, William Proxmire's monthly 'Golden Fleece' award for wastage of public money are these dubious contributions to the stock of human knowledge:

The Law Enforcement Assistance Administration funded a $27,000 investigation into the reasons why inmates wish to escape from prison.

!

The Department of Transportation spent $225,000 on a report forecasting US transportation needs in 2025 under hypothetical conditions of Ice Age, Dictatorship, Hippie Culture and 'American Dream'. Among the valuable findings which emerged were that with an Ice Age there would be a 'significant increase' in population movement southwards, and under Dictatorship, with the consequent urban guerrilla warfare, car insurance premiums might go up.

!

The Law Enforcement Assistance Administration spent $2m developing, and then scrapping, a prototype police car. One of the essential features of the car, developed to improve police efficiency, was a visual indicator on the dashboard that showed whether the siren was on.

!

The National Endowment for the Humanities funded a $2,500 study on why people cheat, lie and are rude on tennis courts.

!

The prestigious Smithsonian Institute contributed $89,000 towards the compilation of a dictionary of the Tzotzil language, an unwritten tongue of Mexican peasants, of whom only 10,000 of the 120,000 total speakers could understand the particular dialect chosen. Since the dictionary gave English translations, few of the 10,000 had any use for it as they mostly spoke only Spanish.

!

Another fruitful area of research would be to discover the value of these recent PhD theses:

Heterosexual coital positions as a reflection of ancient and modern cultural attitudes. (Buffalo, New York)

Funeral games in Greek literature, art and life. (Pennsylvania)

Brazilian Portuguese words and phrases for certain aspects of love and parts of the body. (Wisconsin)

Ancient Greek market regulations and controls. (Berkeley)

The concept of social rage in the Old Testament and the Ancient Near East. (Michigan)

Homosexual tendencies in seagulls. (California)

Discourse particles: an analysis of the role of 'Y'know', 'I mean', 'well', and 'actually', in conversation. (Cambridge)

Powerlessness and meaninglessness amongst graduate students at a university in Oregon. (Oregon)

Suicide among eskimos in Alaska. (Alaska)

Life history characteristics of midges in temporary peat pools. (Dublin)

Melopoeia, phonopoeia, logopoeia and the evolution of Ezra Pound's literary technique. (Manchester)

Bees and beekeeping in classical antiquity. (Leicester)

The gnome and its uses in certain Old English poems. (Oxford)

The influence on their decision-making of the different interpretations of actors involved in the garbage strike and boycott of 1968 at Memphis, Tennessee. (Queen's University, Belfast)

The leg muscles of the adult honey bee. (London)

The effect of two world wars (1914–18 and 1939–45) on poetry composed by the seventeenth-century Marathi saints in Maharashtra. (Bombay)

The correct alignment of various fixtures in the bathroom. (Stockholm)

The Government-funded Economic and Social Research Council (formerly known as the Social Science Research Council) spends millions each year on commissioning research in the social sciences. Among its recent grants are the following, whose ultimate value in the great scheme of things one must judge for oneself:

An analysis of the concept of leisure. (2½ years, £32,694)

An inter-disciplinary approach to the study of conversation. (Swedish exchange visit)

The Lincolnshire clergy in the later fourteenth century. (2 years, £1,145)

Family, friendship and neighbourhood among rural Finns. (1 year, £8,049)

Social organisation of long-distance traders in Libya. (3 years, £18,962)

The social and political implications of household work strategies. (3 years, £98,667)

The development of crying in infancy and its effects on the mother. (3 years, £35,632)

Women and religion in a Turkish town. (4 years, £25,317)

The use of the concept of old age. (1¼ years, £21,450)

Relation of failures in working memory to decline in conversation skills of the elderly. (5 years, £75,046)

An exploratory investigation of the effects of jargon on writing and thinking. (1 year, £9,014)

Exchange rates in late mediaeval Europe. (1½ years, £5,130)

The history and architectural implications of cooperative housekeeping in Britain. (1 year, £21,418)

Community and individual annoyance as a function of traffic noise exposure. (2 years, £38,456)

Illegitimacy levels in Scottish regions, 1660–1770. (1 year, £8,730)

The control and distribution of resources within the household. (2½ years, £34,342)

Religion and women in twentieth-century Greece. (3 years, £35,920)

Economic expansion in the Byzantine Empire. (3 years, £37,350)

The development of conversation. (2 years, £21,862)

Judging the probability of future events. (2 years, £19,686)

The effects of geographical change on home sickness. (1½ years, £18,888)

Identifying and remembering faces. (2 years, £17,060)

A comparison of shopping centre hierarchies, 1968 & 1983. (2 months, £700)

Thirty-five years of transformation in central Turkey. (2 years, £29,380)

The culture of drinking in an English community. (1 year, £21,040)

How closing a topic in conversation is socially managed. (1½ years, £16,710)

The televised behaviour of public figures. ($2\frac{1}{4}$ years, £34,540)

An empirical investigation of household behaviour under uncertainty. (2 years, £24,210)

Patients' comprehension of doctors' instructions. (3 years, £11,650)

The role of television in the family. ($1\frac{1}{2}$ years, £29,990)

Overtaking: driver behaviour and attitudes. (2 years, £20,410)

!

Even if it is worthwhile, any research is still not out of danger. A Cornwall school's science experiment on air pollution in 1983 which involved leaving gelatine culture in dishes to monitor dust settlement was ruined by parish councillors who stubbed their cigarettes out in them during a meeting in the school hall. 'We thought they were ashtrays,' one explained.

!

# TEN

# PRACTICE IMPERFECT

'*(1) The registrar of companies may destroy any documents or other material which he has kept for over ten years and which were, or were comprised in or annexed or attached to, the accounts or annual returns of any company.*
*(2) The registrar shall retain a copy of any documents or other material destroyed in pursuance of subsection (1) above.*'

Section 100, Companies Act 1981

!

In February 1978, a judge in Des Moines, Iowa, dismissed a drunken driving charge against a man whom he ruled to have been too drunk to have consented to the blood alcohol test that proved him inebriated.

!

In March 1979, a Miami judge ordered 950 speeding cases to be held in abeyance after hearing evidence that one police radar unit clocked a palm tree travelling at 86 mph and a brick wall doing better than 50 mph. The judge decided that the system might not be entirely reliable.

!

Similar problems in Silver Springs, Pennsylvania, in June 1982 led the court there to ban radar guns. Police using hair dryers disguised as radars reported improved success in controlling traffic.

!

A Canadian court ruled in September 1980 that God was not a person. The British Columbia Appeal Court was faced with the knotty decision because of the bizarre defence employed on behalf of Morris Davie, of Fort Worth, B.C., who was charged with arson after a forest fire. The crux of the prosecution case was the testimony of a firefighter at the scene who had seen Davie fall to his knees, raise his hands as if in prayer and say, 'O God, please let me get away with it just this time'. Davie's defence rested on his claim that the prayer was a privileged communication meant to be heard by God and no-one else. The lower court accepted the argument, and since there was no other evidence to implicate him, acquitted Davie. The Appeal Court, however, took a different view, rejecting the claim on the grounds that privileged communication could only be between two people, and in an interesting theological debate, ruled that God was not a person. So there it is, official.

!

George Labrash, a San Francisco policeman, lost a lawsuit in February 1982 in which he claimed he was a victim of the curse of Tutankhamen. He said that he had suffered a stroke while guarding the famed golden burial mask during an exhibition of the treasures two years earlier which resulted in him losing his job. His claim for compensation against the Egyptian government for exporting dangerous and hazardous goods was rejected.

!

The Italian Supreme Court ruled in September 1982 that lovemaking in a car was not obscene and illegal – with one proviso: the participants had to ensure that all the windows were well steamed-up or iced-over. After delivering their verdict in the twelve-year appeal battle of a couple found guilty of indecent display, one of the judges confided that the conditions laid down by the court 'shouldn't prove any trouble for a thrill-seeking couple who are enjoying themselves'.

!

A Stornoway sheriff ruled in 1982 that a stomach X-ray produced in court was inadmissible as evidence as it had been obtained without a search warrant.

!

Kansas City judge Donald Mason refused permission to a local Grecophile to change his name from Evans to Xartheohadjimadurokaszamnoupoulis because it would be too long for credit cards or computers.

!

Courts are not all unreasonable. In May 1981, the bench at Downham Market in Norfolk fined a disabled driver £45 for not displaying her disabled parking disc. The fine was to be paid at the rate of 10p a year. The thirty-six-year-old defendant had the first 50 of the 450 years paid for her when a whip-round by solicitors and policemen on duty at the court produced a fiver.

!

A Luton industrial tribunal ruled in November 1976 that a man who had stormed out of his office during an argument shouting, 'You'll never see me again', had effectively resigned.

!

The Tasmanian Court of Appeal dismissed allegations of bias in a magistrate who had called a defendant 'a clown, an idiot, a ratbag, a nut, a clot and a dickhead' during a case. The Appeal Court decided that the magistrate was merely expressing an opinion he had formed of the man.

!

In January 1983, magistrates at Barnsley rejected an application for a certificate for a sports and social club because the building was a fire hazard. There was no fire escape, insufficient fire-fighting equipment and inadequate emergency lighting. The club belonged to the local fire brigade.

!

A judge in a divorce case in Milan in June 1985 ruled that the husband was entitled to visiting rights to see his dog after the wife had been awarded custody of the pet.

!

Milton Avol, a Los Angeles neurosurgeon and property owner, was taken to court by his tenants in June 1985 for failing to maintain his flats in a habitable condition. After hearing of rodent infestation, broken windows, cracked walls and peeling paintwork, Judge Veronica Simmons ordered Avol to spend thirty days in prison followed by thirty days in one of the flats. Handing down judgment, she said, 'This is a classic slumlord situation. If certain landlords feared that they would have to live in the same squalor they imposed on some of their tenants, they just might think twice before allowing their apartments to deteriorate to such a level.'

!

Judge Bertrand Richards stunned the legal and medical worlds in July 1985 with his comments while sentencing a man who appeared in his Bury St Edmunds court on burglary charges. Having heard evidence in mitigation that the man had made seven suicide attempts in recent years, the judge said, 'I wish these people would show more efficiency about these overdoses. How much trouble they would save.'

!

A man who abandoned four puppies in sub-zero temperatures at a rubbish tip in Berlin, New Hampshire, was sentenced in February 1982 to spend two nights of the same treatment.

!

The penalty for adultery in the Indonesian village of Selokajang, on East Java, was settled by the village chief in July 1986 when he fined a man 4,000 bricks for sleeping with a neighbour's wife. The chief explained that the bricks would help to improve the village. He also confiscated the adulterer's bicycle to ensure the safety of nearby villages.

!

In June 1985 the Canadian Supreme Court ruled that all the laws passed since 1890 in the province of Manitoba were 'of no force or effect' because they had been printed only in English and not also in French as required by the terms agreed when Manitoba entered the Canadian federation. 4,500 laws and some 30,000 regulations were thought to be affected, but the court allowed the province to agree a timetable for their translation. For the twenty years it was expected to take, the court ruled that the laws should be deemed to be temporarily valid so that the province would not become totally lawless.

!

Elsewhere in the world, there are many who would wish a similar fate to befall their rulers. Iranian justice is, for example, a delicate creature:

In a literal eye-for-an-eye court case in October 1984, an Islamic judicial panel ruled that twenty-two-year-old Maryam Zaverei should be allowed to gouge the eyes of her husband Taghi. The Tehran couple had separated four years earlier after he had suspected her of infidelity and driven her into the desert where he cut her eyes out with a knife. Court reports said that Mrs Zaverei had chosen her implement, a pair of scissors, and added that the blinding ceremony might be televised nationally. It was later reported that she had successfully carried out her retribution by gouging one eye but had agreed a financial settlement in respect of the other one.

!

In October 1987 it was reported that three child-killers were given the choice, by an Islamic court which had found them guilty, of either being hanged, beheaded or pushed over a cliff. They all elected for the death leap from the cliff, and were granted their wish.

!

As a result of complaints, Iran's leadership ruled in 1981 that men and women mountain climbers must be segregated in future.

!

The sexes rebelled when Tehran city council introduced ordinances segregating men and women on the city's buses. Men had to crowd on the top deck while women sat comfortably below. The scheme was quickly abandoned.

!

During a phase of particular fanaticism in the summer of 1986, so-called 'morality squads' toured Tehran on the lookout for the faintest hint of un-Islamic behaviour. Women were arrested for the offence of wearing lace on their headscarves. Couples were stopped and their relationship queried. The Shi'ite rite of seegheh was enforced requiring temporary marriage – for as little as an hour – before young men could enjoy the company of women.

!

Still, a gleam of justice did creep through. It was reported in February 1979 that a Tehran whipman who miscounted during the punishment of a convicted alcohol drinker was strung up and the victim allowed to give him one back. The victim commented that it was worth all the twenty-six lashes he had been given.

!

Peking traffic regulations ban the use of headlights on cars after dark – in order to prevent cyclists from being dazzled.

!

Under Italian law a woman convicted of minor offences cannot be imprisoned if she is pregnant. When Eliga Spinelli was sentenced to ten months in jail for stealing a chicken in 1975, she successfully avoided it by becoming pregnant. And she has continued to do so by having a child every year since. The Italian press reported her fourteenth consecutive pregnancy in March 1986. As far as is known, she is still going strong.

!

In 1985 the authorities in Niger state in Nigeria introduced an excrutiatingly novel death penalty for convicted armed robbers – the slow execution by firing squad. Condemned prisoners were shot initially in the ankles and then progressively higher up the body at five minute intervals until they were dead. Abubaka Sule, the state's spokesman, said the method of execution was designed to deter would-be offenders and make the guilty suffer for their crimes.

!

An Australian teacher who claimed on his tax form for deductions for depreciation of his brain during the course of the year had his claim rejected by the Tax Office in December 1987. The Office ruled that the ingenuity and complexity of the calculation clearly demonstrated that the teacher's brain capacity had not been adversely affected.

!

The pilot of a light aircraft who thought he was running out of fuel made an emergency landing on a highway in De Kalb, Illinois, in September 1982. A police patrol gave him a ticket for entering at the wrong junction and failing to pay the 30c toll.

!

Dudley Wayne Kyzer was jailed for 10,000 years by a court in Tuscaloosa, Alabama, in 1981 for murdering his wife. He was then sentenced to two life terms for murdering his mother-in-law and a college student.

!

Donald Westerholt was jailed for fifty years in Houston, Texas, in January 1983 for shoplifting a pair of shoes worth $20. 'Houston juries are getting tired of crime,' the prosecutor said.

!

Swedish customs officers found Ulf Adelsohn's excuse that he was unaware that it was illegal to bring into the country the cordless telephone found in his luggage a little difficult to believe when they stopped him in November 1985. As Communications Minister, Mr Adelsohn had been the Minister responsible for drawing up, passing and signing the law which banned the imports.

!

Jackson Martin, of Durant, Oklahoma, was convicted of indecent exposure in February 1982. The jury, comprising nine women and three men, recommended a prison sentence – of ninety-nine years.

!

Keith Allen MP, the chairman of the New Zealand parliamentary committee examining tougher laws against drunken drivers, was convicted and fined on a drink-drive charge after a meeting of the committee in January 1982.

!

A twenty-two-year-old Swede who fitted a lawnmower engine to his roller skates and travelled around Malmo at 17 mph was fined for not having an MOT.

!

John Maule was fined £100 by Newcastle upon Tyne magistrates in September 1984 for driving his company's hearse, complete with corpse-laden coffin, at 102 mph while returning from Manchester.

!

Jagat Singh was jailed for fourteen days at Warley in the West Midlands in February 1983 after admitting his 287th drinking offence.

!

Twenty-seven-year-old Debbie Barrett from Carlsbad, New Mexico, was convicted in October 1982 of shooting and wounding her husband during a domestic dispute. The judge sentenced her to three years at college on the grounds that since she had already qualified for a scholarship, it would be cheaper for the state than keeping her in jail.

!

Shrewsbury magistrates were told during a drink and disorderly case in February 1974 that the accused man was apprehended after trying to climb the ladder he was carrying.

!

A young man in Bodo, Norway, was charged in 1980 for being drunk in charge of a vacuum cleaner – a large hangar cleaner to be exact on which he executed slalom runs between parked aircraft at the local airport.

!

Brisbane police in the suburb of Redcliffe arrested a man for riding a bicycle while under the influence of alcohol. Two years earlier the same police arrested a man for being drunk in charge of a wheelchair.

!

Pauline Facey of Ilkeston was fined £10 in October 1982 for being drunk in charge of a horse.

!

Police in London, Ontario, arrested a drunk in February 1983 for walking in a straight line. He had been walking down the street and came up against the parked patrol car. He stepped onto the bonnet, proceeded over the top and onto the boot, jumping back on the road and continuing on his instinctive way home.

!

In March 1983, West German police arrested an Austrian vagrant for cooking his onion soup over the eternal flame at Berlin's war memorial.

!

Devon County Council roadworkers painting yellow lines along a road in Newton Abbot in May 1982 had their van ticketed by a traffic warden for parking near the still wet markings.

!

In December 1985, an ambulance attending an emergency call in Swindon was booked, flashing lights and all, for illegal standing.

!

Willie Walker retired in April 1983 after sixteen years as a traffic warden in Dumfries. During his career, he had only ever booked one car, and then because a policeman had instructed him to. 'I always found that a friendly word was best,' he said.

!

During a peace protest outside the US air base at Alconbury in October 1982, discretion triumphed over valour when 30-stone Sheila McLaughlin sat down in the road and refused to move. The efforts of the local constabulary were to no avail. Inspector Mays told Huntingdon magistrates that to avoid injury to his officers, he was forced to allow her to remain until she decided to go. Traffic was diverted around her.

!

The fire brigade in the central Swedish town of Orebro were presented with a bill for £100 in December 1982 for parking fines incurred while attending fires. The fire chief refused to pay. 'We haven't got time to put coins in parking meters when we're called out,' he said.

!

A Filipino woman found guilty at London's Marlborough Street magistrates court of shoplifting in December 1980 asked the bench if she would get a discount for paying her fine in cash. Her request was refused.

!

A drugs trial in Newcastle upon Tyne Crown Court in April 1985 came to a brief halt after the defending counsel took too close a look at the prosecution's prize exhibit – a bag containing 8 oz of cannabis resin. After sniffing it intently, he complained of feeling dizzy and had to ask for an adjournment.

!

The Dublin trial of Martin Cahill in October 1981 for alleged theft of silverware was halted when another man sitting in the public gallery interrupted proceedings to announce that he had committed the crime.

!

A London magistrate reported in November 1986 the case of a woman convicted for soliciting who asked for time to pay her fine. The bench asked her how long she needed. 'About twenty minutes should do,' came the reply.

!

In March 1983, Taiwanese bricklayer Hua Ting Kuo was acquitted of murder at the end of his thirteenth trial for the alleged offence. He had been found guilty and sentenced to death on twelve previous occasions.

!

Frank Messina of Franklin, Pennsylvania, lodged a suit against the state Transportation Department in February 1985 for prosecuting him ten years earlier for dangerous driving and causing suspension of his licence. He claimed damages of $5,764,609,563,143,700 and 48 cents on the grounds that his life had been ruined. State officials were confident they would successfully resist. 'Otherwise, there won't be no Pennsylvania anymore,' one said.

!

After suffering a dozen burglaries at his garage in Ville-naux-la-Grande in central France, Lionel Legray assembled a booby-trapped transistor radio packed with explosive to frighten the next thief. He even told the local police of his plan. They did not object provided that he put notices up to warn would-be burglars. The unlucky thirteenth burglar was unfortunately illiterate and the bomb was a little larger than Legray expected. It blew the robber to pieces. Although found guilty of manslaughter and sentenced to eight months, his appeal, which lasted six years, was successful and he was finally exonerated by a court in Troyes in November 1982.

!

The worst prison in the world must be that of the Solomon Islands in the Pacific. In October 1985, all 149 prisoners escaped from the capital's central jail when prison guards went on strike and opened all the gates in protest. They were presumably all recaptured, for less than a year later, in August 1986, it was reported that the prisoners had again escaped, this time after overpowering the guards. Only one, described by the authorities as 'an honest man' refused to escape.

!

Fabio de Angelis, twenty-one, escaped from San Marino's jail in March 1986. There was little excuse – at the time he was its only prisoner.

!

During the Marxist coup on the Caribbean island of Grenada in March 1979, revolutionaries opened the prison gates and released all the inmates. New leader Maurice Bishop, who was disappointed by this demonstration of lawlessness, appealed immediately for all prisoners to return – which they did, except two who gave notice of their intention to spend the night away. Both duly returned the following morning to be locked up.

!

Two prisoners who broke out of Swansea's magistrates court in January 1982 forgot that they were still handcuffed together when they ran either side of a lamppost. After hospital treatment for a broken wrist each, they were remanded back in custody.

!

While on trial in Florence during 1984 for terrorism, Fernando Cesaroni and Maria Pia Cavallo were locked in a cage in court with other defendants. The case, which lasted over a year, took an unexpected turn in February 1985 when Cavallo gave birth to Cesaroni's child. Two court officials were sacked for failing to prevent the fraternisation and the parents were given additional two-month prison sentences for committing obscene acts in public.

!

The authorities at the Bang Khwang prison in Thailand decreed in January 1983 that the fifty-year-old machine gun used for executions should be replaced by a newer weapon with a silencer because the old one 'scared' other inmates.

!

Committed to a prison of a different sort, Norman Green, a forty-two-year-old father of six wanted on suspicion of burglary, evaded the police for eight years by living in a hole 6ft by 2ft under the floorboards of his home in Wigan. Literally going to ground in 1974, Green remained in the hole continuously for the first two years, seeing no daylight and no other person except his wife. When he emerged, he had hair two feet long, his front teeth had fallen out and he was incapable of walking. His children no longer recognised him. After four years, he got himself a mattress to sleep on. 'After the first two years, the police didn't come round so much,' he later said. They eventually discovered the tomb in March 1982. His first words when he was found were, 'Thank God it's over'.

!

# ELEVEN

# ILL TREATMENTS

'*The first few minutes of life can be the most dangerous*' – advertisement for talk on safe childbirth … '*And the last few minutes can be a bit dodgy too*' – Graffiti added, Essex women's club, 1979

'*Among the side effects of the mercurial drug, the most important is the death of the patient shortly after the injection.*'

New York state Medical Journal

'*Caution. Guards Dogs Operating.*'

Sign outside Epsom district hospital, 1978

!

The Chinese press reported in December 1980 that surgeons had removed thirty-five-year-old Zhang Zipang's second head. Zhang, from a mountainous village near Kunming in central China, was born with a parasitic 7½ in second head on his right shoulder. It had an undeveloped brain which did not function and eyes which did not open; otherwise it had normal appearance, with eyebrows, eyelashes, nose, beard, teeth and tongue. Surgeons took eight hours to remove the head. Zhang was said to wish to return home to get married.

!

The American Medical Association reported in May 1979 the case of a twenty-two-year-old Wisconsin University student who performed an eight hour operation on himself. After months of preparation and acquiring appropriate instruments, he disinfected his college room, draped sterilised sheets over his body, swallowed barbiturates for anaesthetic and performed the operation wearing gloves and a surgical mask. Lying on his back with strategically placed mirrors, he opened his abdomen with scalpels and retractors in an attempt to operate on his adrenal glands. He was forced to give up after eight hours when he experienced unexpected pain in retracting his liver. Exhausted, he bandaged his wound, cleaned the room and called the police. When he arrived at hospital, surgeons who examined the wound were astonished at the remarkable cleanliness of the work and impressed by the ligatures tied around the major blood vessels. They closed the wound and he made a full recovery. A doctor later commended the student's technique, but recommended he undergo extensive psychiatric counselling.

!

In May 1976, doctors at the Metropolitan Hospital in New York removed over 500 items from the stomach of a mental patient. Over 300 coins were recovered, along with 30 penknives, 20 keys, half a dozen metal chains, broken thermometers, tin openers, eating utensils, nuts, metal fragments and bolts. The operation took two hours.

!

The *Chinese Daily* reported in early 1982 that doctors in Shanghai had successfully used flesh from a woman's arm to replace her cancerous tongue. It said the patient was able to speak normally.

!

In December 1982, a medical journal reported the case of an unidentified woman who survived and functioned normally with more than three times the recognised lethal level of alcohol in her blood. The twenty-four-year-old Los Angeles girl walked into the California University Medical School saying she had drunk a bottle of Scotch most days for the last six months or so. She had become concerned that she had started to fall over and was suffering from nausea and vomiting. Doctors reported that she was alert but agitated and confused. She answered questions coherently. Tests found her blood alcohol level to be 1510 milligrams/100 millilitres. The drink-drive limit is 80 mg/100 ml, the usual lethal dose 500 mg/100 ml. After two days of treatment, she discharged herself.

!

A Dane who tried to commit suicide in April 1982 by drinking two and a half bottles of Scotch, survived, 'almost miraculously', according to doctors, despite his blood becoming almost one per cent pure alcohol.

!

Twenty-eight-year-old Asif Mohammed from Dundee, suffering from depression in November 1984, chopped both of his feet off. Surgeons later sewed them back on.

!

A Gloucester man whose nose was bitten off during a fight in March 1981 had it sewn back on by surgeons when it was found by police after a search of the pub where the fight took place.

!

Spanish doctors reported in November 1983 the case of Jesus de Frutos, a lorry driver from Segovia, who was suffering acute insomnia, not having slept for nearly thirty years. Thirty-six specialists have failed to find a cure and Sr de Frutos was said to be resigned to spending his nights listening to the radio.

!

After a road accident in 1978, Lincolnshire man Walter Nicholl developed an affliction which caused him to go to sleep every few hours. The condition, sleep apnoea, meant that he needed seven hours sleep during the day as well as a regular turn at night. He tried to sue the other driver in the accident but failed, the judge ruling that the accident had merely accelerated the affliction's onset. The trial itself had to be regularly interrupted by Nicholl's need to go off for a nap.

!

Among other medical curiosities reported from around the world in recent years:

Reports from China in June 1981 hailed five-year-old Liu Debiao as a giant-child. He was already 5 ft tall and weighed 6 st 7 lb, the normal dimensions of a twelve year old.

Abraham Munoz, an eighteen-month-old baby from Murcia, in Spain, was reported in February 1983 to be over 3 ft tall and almost 3 st in weight, the size of a four year old.

Reports from Kashmir in 1982 said that Ghucam Ahmed Dar, twenty-five, had refused financial inducements to join a circus. The smallest man in the country, he measured only 18 inches in height.

A three-legged baby was born in Swaziland, in southern Africa in May 1985. Doctors reported that the extra limb would be amputated after three months and that the boy would lead a normal life.

A two-headed baby girl was born in South Africa in January 1988, but died after forty-eight hours.

An Indonesian woman carried an unborn baby in her womb for eight years. Doctors in Tebing Tinggi, in Sumatra, operated in February 1982 to remove the long-dead foetus which had fossilised.

Philip Taylor from Welwyn Garden City entered hospital in December 1981 after doctors had diagnosed appendicitis. When surgeons began operating they discovered that he did not have an appendix. Doctors put the rarity of the case at 100,000 to 1.

Surgeons in Pakistan removed a 99 lb tumour from the stomach of Rashida Begum in November 1985.

The *British Medical Journal* reported in December 1981 that a 117 lb cyst which weighed more than the rest of the patient had been removed from a British woman.

A ten-year-old Chicago girl gave birth to a healthy 6 lb baby in April 1984. She had no idea that she was pregnant.

!

The *British Medical Journal* reported in 1981 the case of an eighty-five-year-old man who had begun to suffer chest pains in 1979. When doctors examined him, they discovered a shrapnel wound caused sixty-two years earlier during the First World War. A lump of metal a centimetre square was later removed. It was thought to be the longest recorded presence of a foreign body after wounding.

!

A woman who fainted during the bloody guillotine scene in *The Scarlet Pimpernel* at Chichester Theatre in October 1985 passed out for a second time when a helpful first aid worker offered her a tomato juice.

!

Treatment by 'experts' can, however, be an equally risky affair:

In a mix-up at a Government hospital in Bombay in December 1983, doctors carried out an eye operation on a patient who should have had his kidney stone removed, despite his urgent protests that there was nothing wrong with his eyesight. A Parliamentary inquiry decided however that compensation was not appropriate because the eye had not been damaged in the operation.

!

Milorad Jovanic entered hospital in Vienna in September 1982 for treatment for rheumatism. During his stay, he slipped and broke a leg. When it was set he was placed by mistake in a pre-op ward. Soon after he was wheeled into a theatre, strapped to a table and anaesthetised. When he woke up, he discovered that he had had a heart pacemaker fitted. He stayed in hospital a further three weeks to recover from the operation, after which the pacemaker was removed in a second operation. Whether his rheumatism was cured after all this is not recorded.

!

A Florida man, rushed to hospital in 1981 after a snake had bitten him, was told by doctors once the poison had been removed to stick his finger in an ice-pack. Two weeks later the finger had to be amputated because of frostbite.

!

A Chinese newspaper reported in May 1985 the case of a Shanghai factory worker in the city's main hospital who asked a nurse for a drink of water during the night and received a bottle of sulphuric acid by mistake. His condition was reported as 'critical'.

!

A seventy-eight-year-old Tamworth woman was told by her health authority in April 1981 that she had been put on the waiting list for hip-replacement surgery. The list was forty-two-years long. Caroline Pulcella later had the operation after her MP discovered that the health authority in Brechin, Scotland, was able to perform it straight away.

!

Swedish army surgeons adopted a controversial training programme in 1982 to improve battlefield technique. In order to ensure an air of reality, live pigs were systematically subjected to gunshot, grenade and other wounds of varying severity to test the ingenuity of trainee surgeons. The surgeons claimed that Sweden's neutrality meant that very few army doctors had ever had to deal with real military wounds. The spokesman denied cruelty. The animals, he said, were anaesthetised before being wounded. Once the surgeon had practised the operation and post-op procedures to 'save' the animal, it was promptly killed and incinerated without regaining consciousness.

!

The reason for the rising cost of health care in the West German state of Baden Wurttemburg was partially explained in September 1982 when the accounting office revealed that doctors in three university clinics had claimed overtime for working on February 30 and 31. They had also claimed to have worked on the thirty-first day of months which only had thirty.

!

An unnamed fifteen-year-old schoolboy was reported by police in December 1983 to have driven his parents' car twenty-seven miles from Portsmouth to Southampton while still asleep. Officers were called when the boy's father received a phone call at 3.30 in the morning from his son saying he had woken up to find himself in the car. Police located the boy who was confused and distressed and still dressed in pyjamas. Police confirmed that the boy had never driven before but had no reason to disbelieve the story. 'We are taking him to a doctor for treatment for sleepwalking,' Chief Inspector Colin Lewis said.

!

Sixty-five-year-old James McDonnell returned to his home in Larchmont, New York, in December 1985 fifteen years after he had lost his memory in a car accident and disappeared without trace. A second accident in 1985 restored it and he looked up his wife's name in the phone book and went home. He had no recollection of what he had done in the missing fifteen years.

!

Robert Izaguirre, a student from Idaho, shot himself in the leg with his rifle while sleepwalking in February 1985. He only discovered his injuries when he woke up in the morning. He collapsed from shock.

!

An unusual case of double identity was reported in 1980 when identical twins from York, Greta and Freda Chaplin, appeared in court on a minor charge. Court doctors were unable to explain what caused the two 37-year-old women, who dressed and behaved identically, to speak in unison. Throughout the case, the sisters replied to questions simultaneously, and followed identical body movements.

!

A man visiting his brother in a mental hospital in Wellington, New Zealand, in 1982 drove his car up the steps and parked it in the ward. He was detained for psychological reports.

!

Fifty-five-year-old Wallace Rombough suffered a heart attack while driving in Melbourne in June 1982. His car ran out of control and crashed into another driven by Neil Duckworth, President of the Victoria Cardio-Pulmonary Resuscitation Society. Rombough was revived and taken to hospital for observation.

!

A woman who was 'totally convinced' that she was either a lion or a tiger, was arrested in June 1981 after climbing over a safety fence at Dallas zoo and trying to attract leopards. She had removed her shoes and was pushing them into the cage. She was led away after responding positively to a police suggestion that she see a psychiatrist.

!

A woman suffering from a rare psychological disorder ran amok in the Royal Shrewsbury Hospital after being refused admission when she demanded surgery. Assaulting staff and throwing a fire extinguisher and chairs through a window, Susan Jenkins-Hammond was arrested for causing damage. At her trial in October 1982 the court heard that she suffered from Münchhausen's syndrome which generates an impulsive and obsessive wish to enter hospital for surgical operations. She was ordered to undergo psychological tests – and was reported to be overjoyed at the prospect.

!

The Public Health Office in Palermo, Sicily, was ordered by the city council to be shut in March 1982 because it was unsanitary. The toilets did not work, vandals had broken most of the windows and the place was infested with mice.

!

Public health inspectors in Ipswich declared their own staff canteen a health hazard in September 1983 after discovering evidence of rat infestation.

!

The East Essex Health Authority launched a 'Better Health' campaign in the summer of 1986. Publicity was to be adorned with an expensively designed logo showing a cardiogram. Only at the last moment was it realised that the cardiogram showed the patient to be dead.

!

A Japanese recording company produced what it claimed was a remedy for lazy insomniacs as an April Fools' joke in 1983 – an eighty-five minute cassette recording of a monotonous voice counting sheep. It proved so popular – and apparently effective – that a reissue was rushed out within a week.

!

Emmanuel Vitra, the world's longest surviving heart transplant patient finally died in May 1987, aged sixty-seven, some eighteen years after being one of the earliest recipients of a new heart. Known as Mr Indestructible, he even outlived one of the surgeons who performed his operation. *He* died in 1982 – of a heart attack.

!

# TWELVE

# **PARTY GAMES**

'*To promise, pause, prepare, postpone,*
*And end by letting things alone;*
*In short, to earn the people's pay*
*By doing nothing every day.*'
W.M. Praed, on Lord Melbourne's government, 1839

'*I take a balanced view of the government – I like it less than*
*last week, but more than next week.*'
Graffiti, London 1979

!

The allure of Parliament, Praed notwithstanding, is its
unpredictability. For long hours its business is conducted
with monotonous tedium, but deeply embedded amid
the endless columns of *Hansard* are tiny sparklets of
humour, absurdity or just plain rudeness. The task of Mr
Speaker is no easy one. As the House livens up and
passions are aroused, one of the most difficult of his
responsibilities is to ensure that members proceed in a
seemly and gentlemanly way. The realm of the unparliamentary expression is a source of ceaseless controversy.
Mr Speaker's job in deciding what is and is not offensive
to the House is not as simple as it might appear. Obscen-
ities are clearly out, as are imputations of another
Member's lack of honesty – 'liar' is definitely verboten.

Other profanities ruled out over the years have been 'villain' (1875), 'impertinence' (1876), 'ruffianism' (1901), 'murderer' (1923), 'hooligan', 'blackguard' (1922), 'cad' (1924), 'pecksniffian cant' (1928), 'insulting dog' (1930), 'jackass' (1933), and 'swine' (1935).

The rules inevitably have stimulated a beguiling ability to circumvent the spirit of the procedural law. Churchill's 'terminological inexactitude' is perhaps the most famous suggestion that something might not be as had been stated. The story is also told of the young Disraeli, upbraided for calling half the Cabinet asses. 'Mr Speaker, I withdraw,' he apologised. 'Half the Cabinet are not asses.'

A look through the record of more recent years reveals the never-ending battle to see just how far one can go in the heat of debate:

In July 1972, Liberal leader Jeremy Thorpe got away with this, responding to a charge from a Labour member that the Liberal Party 'is like a rocking horse – all motion and no progress'. 'The hon Gentleman is like the grocer's cat – all piss and wind.'

!

In December 1975, Speaker Selwyn Lloyd showed that skilful defusing is as much a part of the job as admonition, when Chancellor of the Exchequer, Denis Healey was interrupted by Labour backbencher, Denis Skinner, during a statement on the economy:

MR HEALEY – If the honourable member will keep his trap shut the whole House will be interested to hear what I have to say. (*Laughter and cheers.*)

175

MR SKINNER – I wonder whether that is an unparliamentary expression.

THE SPEAKER – I do not think asking a member to shut up is unparliamentary. How it is precisely phrased is not a matter for the Chair.

MR SKINNER – I am getting more than a little concerned about the use of language. You will have noticed, Mr Speaker, only yesterday a Secretary of State answering questions with the use of the word 'codswallop', and now the Chancellor of the Exchequer is talking about one keeping one's trap shut. You ought to be doing something about that.

THE SPEAKER – One of the difficulties is that when the Chancellor of the Exchequer is standing where he is, I cannot see whether Mr Skinner's trap is open or shut. (*Loud laughter.*)

!

In June 1985, John Prescott, a Labour frontbencher was able to tell a lady member on the other side of the House she was a 'mean and silly' woman. In November of the same year, the Deputy Speaker ruled that although it was discourteous, Chancellor Nigel Lawson's description of a Labour backbencher as the Shadow Chancellor's 'monkey' was not unparliamentary.

!

Sometimes a spot of negotiating is necessary. Eric Heffer was involved in this exchange in December 1985:

MR HEFFER – Hon Members may say 'Nonsense', but if they and the creeps in the Liberal Party—

THE SPEAKER – Order, I hope the hon Gentleman will rephrase that remark.

MR HEFFER – If the hon Gentleman and the honourable creeps in the Liberal Party—

THE SPEAKER – That is better but not good enough.

MR HEFFER – If I am allowed to say 'crawlers', Mr Speaker, I shall say so.

!

He was. The Speaker ruled in January 1986 that Tony Banks' description of the government as a collection of 'petty crooks' was in order, just. He also allowed in the same month 'buffoon' and did not admonish 'cruel swine' either.

!

The Deputy Speaker drew the line in February 1986 when Alec Woodall tried to enter 'bollocks' on the Parliamentary record. Mr Butterfill's interjection of 'crap' went unchallenged – for a day until it appeared in *Hansard.* The Speaker said he would have ruled it out of order had he heard it. The Member was further anxious to clarify that he had been misreported. He had actually said that the law should be 'scrapped'.

!

Mr Parry called Mr Alton a 'political weasel and gutter-snipe'. Allowed (May 1986).

'Boring old twat' (Mr Cash on Mr Dalyell). Out of order (April 1986).

'Etonian twerp' – (Mr Snape on Nicholas Ridley). Allowed (May 1986).

'Old windbag' (Mr Hamilton on Mr Winterton). Allowed (July 1986).

'Wimp' (Mr Skinner on the Attorney-General). Out of order. The substitute suggested, 'wally', was allowed. (December 1986).

'Bumptious balloon' (Mr Canavan on Chancellor Nigel Lawson). Allowed (December 1987).

!

Parliaments around the world face similar problems. *The Table*, the journal of Commonwealth parliamentary officials, listed in 1984 the following insults which had been ruled out of order during the year:

In India, 'What a donkey you are', and 'nest of cobras', had been outlawed. An Australian member had been brought to book for saying 'It is the best government that money can buy', and another for accusing an opponent of being 'an imperious, arrogant glib toad'. Perhaps the best, and least deserving of censure, was the New Zealand MP's evocative description of his opponents as 'shivers looking for a spine'.

!

Closer to home, in the Parliament of the Isle of Man, the Tynwald (thought to be the oldest continuous legislative assembly in the world), proceedings are conducted with great rectitude. Unparliamentary language is said to be rare. The worst case in recent years was when one member called another a kipper. Asking for an explanation, the bemused recipient was told he was two faced and gutless.

!

Elsewhere, Parliamentary life is anything but peaceful. The Papua New Guinea parliament was suspended in uproar in August 1975 after the police minister stormed across the floor of the House of Assembly and punched an opposition member who had called him a 'pumpkin head'.

!

Congressman Otto Arosomena Gomez, a former President of Ecuador, shot and injured two colleagues during a heated debate in Congress in Quito in October 1980.

!

In June 1982, proceedings of the French National Assembly descended into chaos when a controversial bill on immigration was debated. Debate on the measure, which allowed trade unions to carry on negotiations in the languages of the immigrant workforce (mainly Portuguese, Arabic and Serbo-Croat), was conducted by opponents of the bill in a variety of foreign languages to demonstrate the confusion that would result. The shorthand recorders coped with German and Spanish but sent urgent messages to the Chair when one member began in Chadian. The prospect of a string of obscure African and Caribbean tongues was too much. The Speaker announced that only those contributions made in French would be taken down for posterity. That was enough to call the protest off.

!

A filibuster of a more conventional kind almost wrecked a key bill in the Italian parliament in February 1981. In protest at a police powers measure, the small Radical Party attempted to talk the bill out. Facing strict rules about not reading from briefs, leaning against their desks for support or drinking anything stronger than water, the seventeen members kept the debate going for almost two days before running out of speakers. Pride of place went to Massimo Teodori whose speech lasted 16 hours and 5 minutes, a record in parliamentary history.

!

By comparison, the British record seems a mere throwaway remark. Ivan Lawrence's speech against the fluoridation of water on 6 March 1985 lasted for 4 hours 23 minutes, the longest made in the House chamber this century. He denied his intention had been to bore the Government into submission. 'It was not a filibuster. I wanted the argument against fluoridation of water to go on the record; it just happens to be a rather long argument.'

!

On 9 February 1983, Labour MP John Golding ended a speech which was thought to be the longest in British parliamentary history. Moving an amendment during proceedings in committee on the bill to privatise British Telecom, he spoke uninterrupted for 11 hours 15 minutes.

!

At the opposite end of the spectrum, Lord Mishcon established a record for the shortest parliamentary speech on 14 May 1985. He moved his amendment with the words, 'Why not?'

!

Not every piece of legislation in Parliament is controversial. On 17 January 1986, the Marriage (Wales) Bill passed through all its stages in the Commons without a word of debate. Concerned with removing a loophole about reading marriage banns in Church, it was subjected to more considered treatment by the House of Lords – thirteen minutes on Second Reading. It then passed its remaining stages without debate, becoming one of the least talked-about Acts in history.

!

The situation which every Government Minister dreads happened to William Waldegrave, Arts Minister, on 18 July 1983. During question time he had the rare and dubious honour (for a member of Parliament) of having to admit to the House that he did not know the answer to a question. The briefing given to him by his civil servants ran up to question No. 28, sufficient they thought to cover how far they would reach. Unfortunately, No. 29 arrived. The Minister meekly rose to announce that 'The hon Member will have noticed that my brief runs only up to question twenty-eight —' before his words were drowned in mocking laughter. He offered to take the follow-up question, before he went back to the ministry to roast his advisers.

!

To all politicians, getting the people's vote is the most important task they face. Those in the democracies could take a lesson from behind the Iron Curtain where clearly there is no need for them. In national elections in November 1982, Albania announced that every one of the country's 1,627,968 voters had turned out. 1,627,959 had voted for the ruling party, eight ballot papers had been ruled invalid and one elector had had the temerity to vote against.

!

The result evidently sent alarm bells ringing. In February 1987, Albania announced the results of local elections. This time there had been no negative votes at all, and only one spoiled ballot.

!

The sophisticated lengths to which Communists went to demonstrate popular support had a plausibility which at least showed a modicum of understanding of what the game is about. No mention of election practices could be complete without including the definitive example of electoral fraud – the 1928 Presidential campaign in the African state of Liberia. Demonstrating the truth of the old adage that it is not who votes that counts but who counts the votes, Charles King defeated Thomas Faulkner by an official margin of 600,000 votes. The only problem was that the total electorate of Liberia at the time was only 15,000.

!

Similar problems afflicted President Marcos' last election campaign in the Philippines in February 1986. Reports before the election suggested massive fraud in the registration of voters. One small suburban house in the capital, Manila, was recorded as having 204 people living there. Observers mused on the apparent overcrowding, saying that some ought to move next door where only 147 appeared to live. A remote jungle town returned a voting list that was two and a half times the size of its known population. Not surprisingly Marcos managed to win the election, but the corruption was so transparent that even he was forced to admit 'irregularities'. He left the country within a week of the results for exile in the USA.

!

A different way of attracting a following was adopted by thirty-six-year-old Dora Pezzilli who stood as an Independent Communist candidate in local elections in Italy in June 1983. At her campaign rallies she appeared stark naked, covering her modesty only with a small hand-written poster saying 'Vote for Me'. She lost, although it is said that the election was one of the most enjoyable in living memory.

!

Voters in one constituency in the southern Indian state of Karnataka had a memorable election in February 1985. On arrival at the polling stations they received a ballot paper which was four feet long and two feet wide. A record 301 candidates were contesting the seat.

!

Voting is of course only part of an election. Taking part is often more important than winning, an unrivalled opportunity to parade one's prejudices before the public. Californian Lowell Darling announced in 1981 his intention to run for the Presidency in 1984. Having declared his programme, he promptly disappeared into obscurity but leaving this tempting view of life under his rule. He promised to bring 'common sense' back to American politics. The US would resign as a world power and become an international recreation park. Murderers would be forced to eat the people they killed. He planned to abolish parking tickets; instead drivers would be encouraged to park their cars permanently on the logical grounds that the longer they weren't used, the better for the environment. His foreign policy? All nations would be cut apart at their borders and the polar ice-caps would be melted. As the oceans rose, countries would be free to float around and choose their own neighbours.

!

Elections are all about promises, perhaps more than some care to remember. The past caught up with one candidate in Tonga's general election in 1981. In the course of her campaign she said that if she won she would donate all her salary as an MP to charity. She won against all expectations, and served three years without pay. It is not recorded whether she stood again.

!

One MP who paid a greater price in the course of honouring his parliamentary obligations was Victor Biaka-Boda, who for fourteen months represented the

French African colony of Ivory Coast in the Paris senate. In January 1950, he embarked on a tour of the hinterland to discuss with his constituents their concerns – one of which may well have been the food supply. They reportedly ate him.

!

Perhaps they did not know who he was. Politicians need to put a lot of faith in the electorate. It is not always clear that they are wise to do so. In January 1982 the West German Emnid Institute conducted a routine popularity survey of the country's political leaders. 'Minister Meyers', a fictitious candidate, finished sixth, ahead of the Interior and Defence Ministers.

'Contrary to the assumptions of politicians and opinion pollsters, large sections of the population have a high degree of ignorance about politics' an Institute spokesman commented.

!

For some people, politics is too important to be left to the politicians. For them, direct action is the only way to get one's message across. The commitment though is not always to be found in abundance. In Jerusalem in June 1981, the first mass rally of the Committee of Citizens for Action Now had to be postponed for lack of a quorum.

!

Nor is it always accurately channelled. A peace protest outside the American Air Force base at Alconbury in Cambridgeshire in September 1982 aimed to bring the entire base to a standstill. Unfortunately, all 2,500 servicemen were off duty on their Labour Day public holiday.

!

Protest can be eyecatching though. On the twentieth anniversary of the erection of the Berlin Wall in 1981, demonstrators in Hamburg bricked up the entrance to the Soviet airline Aeroflot office. In April 1983, Indian civil servants demonstrated through the streets of New Delhi dressed only in their underwear. They were complaining against the poor quality of the cotton uniforms. Only men were asked to take part.

!

It can also be just plain silly. The Fruitarian Network, a New York based conservationist group launched a campaign in July 1983 urging homeowners not to mow their lawns because of the pain it caused each blade of grass. Nellie Shriver, leader of the 'plant rights committee', said the campaign advocated non-violence towards all living things, including grass. 'It is impossible to cut grass without hurting it,' she said. 'We believe grass has some sort of consciousness, that it has feelings.' The Network claimed a following of some 6,000 vegetarians in New York alone.

!

The urge to organise produces interest groups of all kinds. Street beggars in Nigeria have their own representative organisation. In the northern state of Sokoto, the Sokoto Destitutes Association voted at an emergency meeting in November 1986 to refuse to accept small coins from benevolents as a protest against the federal government's devaluation measures.

!

A group of black academics who established the Association of African, Caribbean and Asian Academics in November 1983 to combat racism in institutions of higher education in Britain announced that whites would be excluded from membership.

!

In many parts of the world fiction more closely mirrors truth than governments would like to admit. In countries where humour used to be the only recourse for expression of opinion, the political joke assumed an importance way beyond its intrinsic value. It provided the most incisive comment on the vagaries and unconventional ways of life in closed societies. We conclude this look at politics with some of the best insights of recent years:

A story circulating Bucharest in the seventies had Romanian strongman Nicolae Ceauşescu disguising himself one night and going out into the bars of his capital to see what his people really thought of him. 'What do you think of Ceauşescu?' he asked a man. The man looked round and whispered, 'I can't tell you here.' They went outside. 'Now tell me what you think of Ceauşescu.' 'Not here,' said the man, anxiously looking around. So they got into a car and drove. Ceauşescu asks again, but the man points to the driver. Finally they are out in the country. They stop the car and walk into the middle of a field. 'Now,' says Ceauşescu, 'what do you think of Ceauşescu?' Still unsure of himself, the man looks round once more before whispering in his ear, 'I like him.'

!

During the later Brezhnev years, the story was told of the President leaving Moscow for another bout of treatment for illness. He tells his understudy to solve the housing shortage, stop the people drinking and end praying. He had a month to achieve it. The first sight on his return was a sign 'Rooms vacant'. There wasn't a drunk to be seen in Red Square and an old lady was looking into a church shaking her fist. He rushed to the Kremlin where his understudy was looking pleased with himself. Even Brezhnev was impressed and asked how he had done it. 'Since you went away, I opened the frontiers and so many people have left there are lots of empty flats. I cut the price of vodka and we have buried all the alcoholics.' 'But,' says Brezhnev, 'what about the old woman at the church?' 'I sent orders to remove all the holy icons and replace them with pictures of our leaders.'

!

It is said that Russian security men always go round in threes. There is one who can read, one who can write and the third to keep an eye on these two dangerous intellectuals.

!

Comrade Goldstein goes to the local party offices to ask for a permit to emigrate to Israel. The official in charge is astonished. 'Haven't you just been appointed party secretary in your village?'

'Oh, I can't complain,' he replies.

'Didn't the party treat you well in every respect?'

'I can't complain.'

'Haven't you got everything you want and need?'

'I can't complain.'

'Then why on earth do you want to go to Israel?'

'Because there I can complain.'

!

Brezhnev arrives in Luxembourg for an official visit. He is met at the airport by the reigning Duke who proceeds to introduce him to his ministers. When the Defence Minister is presented, Brezhnev laughs out loud. 'What does a small country like yours want with a Defence Minister?' he jokes. The Duke is offended and tells Brezhnev that he should respect the courtesies afforded him. 'After all,' he said, 'when I came to your country, I did not laugh when you presented me to your Minister of Justice.'

!

An American visitor boasts to his Russian host that he is so free that he can stand in front of the White House and shout 'To hell with Ronald Reagan'. The Russian replies, 'That's nothing. I can stand in front of the Kremlin and shout "To hell with Ronald Reagan".'

!

The foreman in charge of building a new river bridge in Czechoslovakia was asked if he had any ideas about how its load-bearing capacity should be tested. 'I think we should get fifty lorry loads of Russian troops to drive across it,' he said. 'If it holds, we'll know it's a good bridge, and if it doesn't, an even better one.'

!

The political and economic turbulence in Poland in the early eighties was a rich source of perceptive wit. When martial law was proclaimed in December 1981, all official news broadcasts on Polish TV were read by uniformed army officers. Their green outfits soon meant that news time became known as 'The Muppet Show', because it was introduced by someone in green who talked rubbish and told fairy tales.

!

The 11 p.m. curfew gave rise to black humour. A policeman stops a citizen one minute before curfew time, checks his documents, then pulls out his gun and shoots the man. The policeman's colleague asks him why he did it. It wasn't curfew time yet. 'Yes, but I know where he lived and he didn't have a snowball's chance in hell of making it home in time.'

!

A man walking his dog after curfew is caught without his documents. He tells the police officer where he lives. The concierge would verify him. He is taken to the station while the police check his story. He is later told that she flatly denied knowing him. After a week's interrogation, he is finally released. He arrives home to a beaming concierge who tells him: 'You owe me a bottle of vodka because I saved you. They came after you three times, but I swore blind ...'

!

A man is sent by his wife to look for some meat. He finds only long queues or empty shelves. In the last shop he loses his temper. He curses butchers, communists, Russians and storms out. He hasn't got far when he feels a hand on his shoulder and a blank-faced man says to him: 'Citizen, you said some dangerous things in there. You know what happened in the old days. Bang, bang, and it would have been all over, but we do things differently now. This is a warning.' The man runs home to his wife who asks him if he found any meat. 'My dear, it is far more serious than that; now they have run out of ammunition.'

!

What are the four things wrong with Soviet agriculture? Spring, summer, autumn and winter.

!

Why is Cuba the biggest country in the world? Because it has its troops in Angola, its population in Florida and its capital in Moscow.

!

A man goes into a bank in Warsaw and hands over a suitcase full of banknotes in payment for his new Polski Fiat car. 'Can you tell me when I can pick it up?' he asks.

'You know perfectly well it will not be available until 1996.'

'Yes, yes, but when in 1996,' the man enquires.

'April, I think,' replies the teller.

'But when in April?' he persists.

'Sir, there is a very long queue. It is many years away … I think 25 April.'

'Yes, but at what time?'

'Please. What difference can it possibly make?' says the teller, losing patience.

'It's just that I'm expecting the plumber at 9.15 that day.'

!

Two Russian skeletons meeting. One asks the other, 'Did you die before or after the price rises?'

'Before. What about you?'

'What do you mean? I'm still alive.'

!

# THIRTEEN

# BALLS UP

'*Exercise is bunk. If you are healthy, you don't need it; if you are sick, you shouldn't take it.*'

Henry Ford (attr.)

'*Serious sport has nothing to do with fair play. It is bound up with hatred, jealousy, boastfulness, disregard of all rules and sadistic pleasure in witnessing violence; in other words, it is war minus the shooting.*'

George Orwell, 1950

'*There is an unwritten law in rugby that you never tread on the head of a player if you can avoid it.*'

Chris Ralston, 1979

!

A 'friendly' soccer match in December 1984 between French clubs Barbazon and Portugais was abandoned after turning into a brawl involving all the players, officials and most of the fifty spectators. Police using tear gas eventually brought proceedings to a close. The trouble had started when the referee sent off two players in an effort to calm tension.

!

A Cheshire soccer cup tie was called off before half-time in March 1981 after play became so violent that the referee feared for the safety of the players. When a brawl broke out in mid-pitch the match between Ellesmere Port and Runcorn was abandoned. Both teams were from local police forces and were competing for the Cheshire Chief Constable's Cup. An embarrassed police spokesman later said that all twenty-two officers would be considered for disciplinary action.

!

A local league match between two Devon teams, Braunton and Bradworthy, in 1981 ended early when the referee sent off all twenty-two players after a violent battle was fought with fists on the pitch. For good measure, the referee also booked the two linesmen for joining in.

!

In protest at the suspension of four of their colleagues in November 1984, players of the French third division rugby team from Vergt in the Dordogne played their next match with only eleven players, four short. They also refused to compete for the ball and failed to offer any resistance to the opposition, Gujan Mestras. They lost by a record score for a first-class game, 236–0. The following weekend, their protest continued, Vergt going down by another record, 350–0.

!

A friendly rugby match in 1982 between Devon side Crediton and visitors Coombe Down from Somerset ended less than amicably when the home side scored a disputed try to win the game. In reporting the club to the County Rugby Union, the visitors complained about the less than adequate linesman who allegedly failed to spot the Crediton player carrying the ball stepping out of play during his rush to the line. The reason? At the time, the linesman was involved in a passionate embrace with his girlfriend in the stand some distance away. 'It was their own fault,' a Crediton official was reported as saying unsympathetically. 'They turned up without a linesman so we had to find one for them. It was their bad luck that it just happened to be someone who was so obviously very much in love.'

!

In April 1986, Fourth Division Swindon Town celebrated becoming the first league club to win promotion that season by beating Chester 4–2. The match was more notable however for the fastest booking in soccer history when Chester centre forward Steve Johnson was cautioned for a foul after just two seconds of the game.

!

Coleridge football club from Cambridge appeared in the 1984 edition of the *Guinness Book of Records* as the cleanest side in the country, not having a player booked since they were formed in 1954. The record ended the weekend before the book was published when it had two players cautioned within twelve minutes.

!

Francisco Espia, a twenty-one-year-old Madrid matador became only the second bullfighter in Spain's history to be thrown out of the ring for being drunk in charge of his bull. First-day nerves in July 1983 had, it seemed, tempted him into a local bar prior to his fight. Two hours later, his nerves steadied but little else, he tottered into the ring where he proceeded to remove his shoes and wave them at the perplexed bull. Police removed him, swaying with his red cape, for his own safety and promptly breathalysed him. The authorities were said to be unsure about their powers to charge him for ruining the crowd's entertainment. There appeared to be no provision against fighting a bull drunk – 'common sense, not law, is usually sufficient protection', one official said.

!

Ten-year-old Andrew Williamson was expelled from his Montrose amateur athletic club in August 1985 because he competed in the local highland games and won 10p worth of sweets in a 60 metre race. Officials of the club decreed that the boy's 'earnings' constituted profession-alism and ruled him out of amateur competition.

!

A 1981 Los Angeles police report recorded the booking of a youth for travelling down a steep slope at 116 kmh – on his skateboard.

!

Peter Kippie, a Scottish snooker champion, forfeited his match in the World Amateur Championships in Calgary, Canada, in 1982 – for failing to wear a tie.

!

A gymnastically inclined sentry at an air force base in Greece caused a diplomatic flutter in February 1981 while guarding a flight of four French Mirage jets which landed to refuel en route to Iraq. A feature of the multi-million pound fighter is its long, tapering nose cone. The bored sentry found the temptation too much, hauled himself up and began swinging on the cone for exercise. To his horror, the cone bent gently into an unsightly curve. Unsuccessful in trying to straighten it out, there was only one thing for it. A series of deft swings on the planes parked alongside and soon all four had similar kinks. 'I hoped nobody would notice the difference,' he said later. Four new cones had to be flown out from France before the planes could continue their journey.

!

The international soccer fixture between West Germany and Yugoslavia in June 1983 was almost called off before a ball had been kicked when the military band of honour played the wrong national anthem. Yugoslav players staged an impromptu strike when the band struck up the old royalist anthem. The game was saved by an expatriate taxi driver who happened to be in the stadium. He produced a tape recording of the up-to-date tune. The Yugoslavs still lost, 4–2.

!

Parachutist Charles Amirault of Halifax, Nova Scotia, escaped with a broken shoulder when he fell 8,500 feet and bounced off a petrol station roof after his lines had become entangled during an air display in September 1982.

!

Brazilian soccer side Nacional suffered a rapid increase in on-field injuries at the beginning of the 1984 season when the club hired an attractive nineteen-year-old female called Angela as its masseuse. Ignoring official reprimands from referees for timewasting, the club decided to give her an assistant. Officials said it would help them attract new players despite the low pay.

!

The tiny African state of Swaziland took a gigantic leap into the twentieth century in September 1983 when the national football association banned the use of witch doctors in assisting sides towards victory. A long tradition of the game here, each team regularly employed the services of a local magician to concoct a *muti*, a magic mix which when spread along the team's goal-line was deemed to help keep the ball out. The opposing team would deploy a similar counter-cocktail in their goal. Now the practice is outlawed and teams face a £300 fine for contravening the ban. Joe Mhleko, the secretary of the Swazi FA explained, 'The sight of spectators and even players trying to remove their opponents' *muti* by urinating in each other's goalmouth is becoming very embarrassing to Swaziland.'

!

When Cameroon from West Africa reached the finals of the World Cup in Spain in 1982, they were alleged to have prepared with the help of local witch doctors. In Peru, their opponents in their opening match, a local clairvoyant conducted an all-night seance to counter the black magic. Isidro Samaniego Dios reported that he had transported himself to the stadium where Peru were due to meet Cameroon. 'I called up their spirits and we fought a terrible struggle. But now I've got them safely bottled up. Until we intervened, they had their victory assured.' It didn't look like that when the football started. Cameroon surprised everyone by holding Peru to a 0–0 draw and then went on to hold Poland by the same score in their next match. They even scored a goal against mighty Italy, the eventual tournament winners, and held them 1–1. Italy in fact only qualified for the later stage of the competition by virtue of scoring one goal more than Cameroon. Peru, by contrast, for all its spiritual help finished bottom of the group without a win.

!

Trevor Cox from Cradley, near Birmingham, required hospital treatment during a fishing tournament in January 1986 after catching his hook on the end of his nose.

!

Police were called to break up a brawl during a dominoes tournament in Sunderland in 1981 after it was discovered that the winner had used pieces with removable dots.

!

Pedre Brinaru, a Romanian competitor in the marathon at the 1982 Balkan Games in Bucharest was disqualified for hitching a lift for four miles of the race. He was dropped near the stadium and ran in to take the silver medal.

!

The semifinal of the African Champions Cup in 1984 between Ibadan Shooting Stars of Nigeria and Semassi Sokoda of nearby Togo, introduced a novel variation of supporters' techniques for putting opponents off their play. During the deciding leg in Togo, home fans bombarded the Ibadan team as they emerged from the dressing room with showers of itching powder. All to no avail, though. The Nigerians won.

!

After watching his favourite side Sheffield Wednesday draw 2–2 with Southend in a FA Cup tie in January 1983, life-long supporter Bob Montgomery complained to the South Yorkshire Consumer Protection Department claiming that Wednesday had played so badly that they contravened the Trades Description Act. He claimed that the club had obtained his £3.50 admission money under false pretences. 'This performance was the last straw,' he said and threatened to take the club to court himself. The Consumer Protection Department held out little hope of obtaining sufficient impartial evidence to support the case.

!

The 1985 African Women's basketball championship final between Senegal and Zaire ended in a brawl even before it had started, as Zaire officials protested at the Senegalese team sprinkling 'magic powder' over the Zaire players during the pre-match warm-up. Zaire refused to play and Senegal took the title by default.

!

Before the start of Naples' opening match of the 1985 league season against Como, police confiscated the usual array of items from fans as they entered the stadium. Their haul that day included, in addition to the fireworks and knives, two hand grenades.

!

Doug Hurrell of Essex soccer team Rainsford Eagles set some sort of record in April 1982 by scoring five own goals in one match. Normally a striker, Hurrell played in defence because of a hampering injury in the game against Heybridge Social Club. He deflected two goals past his keeper in the first half, and completed his hat trick early in the second. A header made number four and minutes before the end he sliced a clearance for his fifth. Rainsford lost 13-3.

!

Turkish first division side Orduspor awarded their goal-keeper a £40 bonus after he had conceded four goals in a match in 1980. The club chairman later explained, 'We expected to lose by at least ten goals.'

!

The plight of an English goalie gained national headlines in 1981. Dean Colling of the St Ann's Wanderers, from Nottingham, ran off the pitch and disappeared after letting in 10 goals. The team, which in 15 games had scored only 21 goals and conceded over 200, launched an appeal over local radio for his return. Three weeks later he came back when the team promised to give more effort to their game. His first match augured well since they were due to play the Cotgrave Colts, who arguably had an even worse record than St Ann's, never having won a game. Hopes were soon dashed – the Colts romped home 7–1.

!

Warwickshire pace bowler Gladstone Small wrote himself into the odd records book on 14 August 1982 in the game against Middlesex. He took eighteen balls to complete one over. He bowled eleven no balls in the first three deliveries. Slowing down to half pace to retrieve control, he promptly bowled a wide.

!

The cricket team from the Yorkshire village of Cawood achieved a unique feat in August 1979 by winning a match without scoring a run off the bat. Having bowled out their opponents, Dringhouse, for only two runs, Cawood opener Peter Wright let the first ball of the innings sail past him. Alas, so did the Dringhouse wicketkeeper. It ran to the boundary for four byes. The MCC announced that it had no previous record of a similar occurrence.

!

In September 1984 the Royal Southern Yacht Club from Hamble, Hampshire, won one of the more bizarre cricket matches beating the Island Sailing Club from the Isle of Wight – on a sand bank in the middle of the Solent. Low tides expose the bank for barely an hour each year, and on this occasion just enough time for Royal Southern to bowl out their opponents for twenty-four runs. On the undulating surface and numerous ponds, in which two balls were lost, and watched by the odd passing ferry, the winning runs were knocked up with six wickets, and precious few minutes, to spare before the participants sought refuge in their boats.

!

Reports from around the country in 1985 illustrated some of the pitfalls which face the organisers of amateur rugby clubs. A Sutton Coldfield team playing away in the country took the field just as a groundsman was seen chasing a pig off it. Unfortunately, one of the visitors was a devout Muslim and refused to play on the ground now sullied by the pig. After long negotiations with his captain, a compromise was eventually agreed. He would play, provided that no-one told his parents.

!

A match controlled by a Worthing referee was played with the minimum of stoppages after the whistle became caked in cow dung when he fell over on a more than usually pastural pitch.

!

A game at Shirley was stopped when the home side's tea lady strode onto the pitch during play demanding the key to the kitchen cupboard from the hooker. She became perilously involved in a maul before the referee called a temporary halt to allow the hooker off the field to look for the key. Ten minutes later the game resumed.

!

Carefree enthusiasm in an emergency almost resulted in serious injury when a player in a match at Pershore injured his leg. Keen helpers quickly began to splint the leg with an old length of skirting board. As the bandage was tightened, the player screamed in agony. Two large nails were being driven into his leg as he became nailed to the splint.

!

When a player on a remote Dartmoor pitch broke his leg, he was carried to hospital by his colleagues splinted to a complete five-barred gate.

!

In December 1985, Craig Bodzianowski became the first boxer in the sport's history to fight a bout with an artificial leg. Eighteen months after a car accident which resulted in the amputation, he marked his comeback to the ring in Palos Height, Illinois and won in two rounds.

!

The usually somnolent world of bridge was electrified in April 1987 by the report from a club in Newton Abbot, Devon, of the possibly unique occurrence of all four players being dealt an entire suit of cards in their hand. The chances of such a hand are one in 2,235 billion billion.

!

There is a time and a place ... It was reported in 1982 that a fitness fanatic's obsession with jogging led to a major alert during a transatlantic flight which was forced to prepare for an emergency landing when the aircraft developed sudden and worrying vibrations. The cause was traced to a passenger doing an hour's running on the spot in one of the lavatories.

!

If sport is about anything it is about dedication and determination. No finer example can there be – and a last testimony to all sporting men and women who weekly risk life, limb and ego – than the lady golfer, whose name is sadly lost to posterity, who finished last in the 1912 Shawnee Invitational for Ladies held in Pennsylvania. Her round had been unexceptional until the sixteenth when her tee shot landed in a nearby river. She opted to play the ball and launched herself out in a rowing board. By the time she had splashed the ball out of the water, recovered successively from dense woodland, brush, a sand trap and thick rough, she finally holed out – in a world record for one hole of 166 strokes.

!

# FOURTEEN

# FARCE AND FURIOUS

'*British railways are used by all classes of the community. If you stand and watch commuters arriving at any of the London termini, you will see for yourself that they are a cross section of the population.*'
Travelling in Britain, New York travel guide, 1980

'*During peak periods, the 202 to Heathrow will run every 30 minutes. The rest of the day, it will run half-hourly.*'
Bus information sign, Twickenham, 1986

'*Concorde is great. It gives you three extra hours to find your luggage.*'
Bob Hope, 1976

'*God give me patience – but hurry.*
Graffiti, London, 1985

**!**

British public transport may give a very good impression that it is ceaselessly engaged in a struggle to be the world's worst. It will come as no solace to know that much greater mayhem is required before it can challenge the most celebrated target of travellers' wrath – the state rail network of Victoria, Australia, VicRail. Never heard of it? They certainly don't go out of their way to publicise themselves, but the friendly folk of Melbourne have cause every day to approach their journey to work with apprehension. The city's evening newspaper has a permanent competition for the best 'VicWail', and the company itself has admitted to receiving 900 complaints about its services in one two-month period – for an area perhaps a tenth the size of London.

In the Australian edition of the *Guinness Book of Records*, VicRail has the honour of running the nation's most unpunctual train. The ill-fated 8.08 a.m. from Essendon in the northern suburbs to the city achieved a 97 per cent record for late starting in the period March–August 1978.

The most notorious adventure of recent years occurred on a Sunday afternoon in March 1979. Passengers who boarded the 1.25 p.m. from Spencer Street in the city to the bayside town of Geelong, forty-five miles and an hour's journey away to the south west, were treated to a tour of the northern suburbs when the train took off in the wrong direction. It continued northwards for an hour before signallers managed to contact the driver. An improvised escape route was devised, but the train was misdirected once again in the western suburbs as it tried to re-link with the Geelong line. It eventually reached its destination after an epic three hours and twenty minutes. No explanation was ever proffered for the diversion.

During the state election campaign in March 1982, the Transport minister decided to canvass a Geelong–Melbourne commuter service. The train failed to stop at Werribee, the only intermediate station, taking a dozen passengers on to Melbourne who did not want to go that far. Passengers waiting on the Werribee platform appeared stunned, reports said, as the train hurtled past.

The Minister saw one consolation – 'We did arrive in Melbourne two minutes early.'

Those on board the commuter special from the country satellite town of Bacchus Marsh in December 1981 had travelled only two minutes when the train slowed, then stopped on a long curve. Curious passengers peered out of windows to see the engine steaming off without them. It came back ten minutes later, rejoined itself, and continued the journey. No explanation was offered.

A Melbourne to Eltham service, running express between two suburban stations, made an unscheduled stop in December 1981. A waiting commuter took the unexpected advantage and climbed on. Footsteps followed along the platform and the stationmaster's voice sternly enquired, 'Did anyone get on here?' 'Er, yes. I did,' the passenger said. 'Well, you'll have to get off. This train isn't supposed to stop here.' The man was obliged to leave the train before the guard allowed it to go.

For months, a service left Spencer Street station each afternoon with a spotlessly clean first-class compartment. There was good reason for its cleanliness: it was always empty throughout its journey. It was empty because no-one could get into it without a first-class ticket, and no-one could get a first-class ticket because VicRail had decided to abolish first-class travel in its new fare system. As travellers crowded into the second-class carriages, and brave intruders into the first-class seats were turfed out by guards, complaints mounted until VicRail admitted that there was a problem. A memo was despatched from head office instructing that the first-class carriage be securely locked on all subsequent journeys.

Early in 1981 VicRail inaugurated a $200m (£120m) modernisation programme to phase out Melbourne's ancient 'red rattler' trains in favour of a fleet of luxurious, air-conditioned silver Supertrains. A year later the scheme faced the axe after initial trials of the new trains showed that their reliability was no better than the sixty-year-old engines they were due to replace.

VicRail's modernisation plans were frequently spectacular, but not for the reasons hoped. The new fare structure meant that new style tickets were needed. VicRail under-ordered. For three months stations kept running out of the new tickets and could not get fresh supplies. Passengers were entrusted to pay their proper fares at their destinations.

In June 1982, VicRail finished a $55,000 (£35,000) project to upgrade level crossing signals on a country line. Impressive flashing lights were installed and an automatic barrier was erected. Three days later, according to a plan agreed months earlier, they closed the line. The signals were never used.

!

British Rail clearly enjoys competing. When Southern Region planners decided in January 1983 to reduce the number of stops on local Sunday services, the message failed to get through to all corners of the region. Unaware of the changes, passengers who tried to board the train which drew into Hamble station in Hampshire on the first day of the new arrangements were greeted by a guard who politely informed them that he had stopped the train only to tell them that it no longer stopped there on Sundays. 'If you want to catch the train, you have to walk to Netley,' the next station, a mile away, he said. Refusing to allow anyone to board, on the grounds that officially he wasn't there, he said, 'I'm only trying to be helpful,' as the empty train pulled out.

!

The *New York Times* reported in 1980 that two commuters were arrested after a demonstration by passengers 'when their train left Pennsylvania station at 6.26 p.m., three minutes behind schedule'.

!

Looking after the pennies ... in November 1982, New York police mounted a major operation against commuter fraudsters who had discovered a loophole in the subway's automated slot machines. Passengers had been quick to find that the 17 cent token for a toll road in nearby Connecticut was the same size as the 75 cent token for the New York subway. On the first day of the operation, a hundred or so unsuspecting fiddlers had been caught. On the same day in New York, there were 6 murders, 76 rapes and 2,000 robberies.

!

The hazards of spending a penny can be equally harsh. In 1979, a sign appeared on the only waiting room on Manningtree station in deepest Essex: 'This waiting room is out of use until further notice as someone has stolen the door handle.'

!

In October 1977, an Indian Railways express on the 150 mile run between Ambala and New Delhi killed nine people in nine separate incidents as they tried to cross the track – and it didn't stop once.

!

The Oxford and South Midlands bus company's new timetable introduced in November 1982 allowed villagers in Finstock a bare three minutes to do their shopping. The first bus to the neighbouring town of Charlesbury where the local store is was timed to arrive at 11.38 a.m. The last one back to Finstock departed at 11.41 a.m.

!

A driver on the M5 motorway near Cheltenham in February 1987 stopped his car in the fast lane and began to change a burst tyre. The accident he caused when a car and a coach crashed into his vehicle left wreckage over all three lanes of his carriageway and most of the opposite side too.

!

Police in Chesapeake, Virginia, stopped a weaving car in April 1985 to find it being driven by a twenty-four-year-old blind man. The drunk passenger, who had been giving him directions, had fallen asleep.

!

In July 1986, partially-blind William Bowen of Louisville, Kentucky, who trained his guide dog to sit in the passenger seat of his car and bark to tell him the colour of traffic lights, was sentenced to thirty days in jail for reckless driving after police had stopped his car in view of its erratic steering. In mitigation, Bowen explained that Sir Anheuser Busch, or Bud for short, was still being trained to watch the white lines dividing the lanes.

!

In March 1983 Ruth Jarvis, a newly qualified road safety instructor, was late for her first appointment on her first day in the job when her car collided with a lorry on the way to a demonstration in Bristol.

!

Residents of a Pennsylvania town were reported in 1980 to have devised a failsafe way of persuading motorists to slow down as they entered the built-up area along a notoriously dangerous road. A sign had been erected: 'Caution – Nudists Crossing.'

!

Newham Borough Council recalled a road safety poster it issued as part of a campaign in 1981 after complaints from women's groups about the slogan to encourage the wearing of seat belts – 'Drivers, belt the wife and kids and keep them quiet'. A spokesman accepted that there was probably a better form of words to get the message across.

!

South Yorkshire police reported in March 1979 that one of their patrols had stopped a car travelling sedately up the M1 on the hard shoulder. The two elderly lady occupants explained that they hated using the motorway and were convinced that it was safer to travel on the hard shoulder. They had one complaint, however. It was tedious having to leave the motorway at each junction. They loyally followed the hard shoulder off at each intersection, went around the roundabout and rejoined the motorway on the other side.

!

The complexities of the freeway system near Tampa Bay airport in Florida were too much for eighty-seven-year-old Jack Comiskey and his seventy-three-year-old wife Winifred when they arrived from Chicago for a holiday in April 1985. Driving off in their rental car, they mistook the airport's runway for the town-bound motorway and sped off across the tarmac until they came to the end of the landing strip and plunged into a safety lake at 50 mph. A plane coming into land was waved away at the last moment. The couple were unhurt. The wife said later that she thought the road was a little quiet. 'There was nothing behind us and nothing coming the other way.'

!

The cause of a four-hour traffic holdup on the M27 near Southampton on 27 July 1986 was a police accident prevention caravan which had overturned blocking two lanes of the carriageway.

!

Traffic in the Kent town of Strood came to a standstill during the festive season in 1982 when the town's traders committee switched on the Christmas lights in the high street. A myriad of snowflakes, hung from lamp-posts at head height began to flash ... red, orange and green in colourful opposition to the traffic lights. After one night the lights had to be turned off. The town had bought the lights from nearby Gillingham, where the previous year they had been a great success. Unfortunately, no-one had thought of the significance of the fact that Gillingham's high street was pedestrianised.

!

There is only one set of traffic lights on the island of Malta, and they have been permanently switched off since 1983. The assistant commissioner of police explained that the lights themselves were in perfect working order. 'The only problem is that when we switched them on, no-one took any notice so we switched them off to save electricity.'

!

And when Ghana gained independence in 1957, the country's leading newspaper proudly announced that the capital's first set of lights were 'in the national colours, red, yellow and green'.

!

Some years ago, parish councillors in the Sussex village of Horam decided to take action after a number of cars had knocked down the name sign on the roadside at the entrance to the village. In future, it would be located directly behind a large oak tree. 'Nobody's likely to see it now,' a spokesman said in explanation, 'and they'd have to hit the tree first anyway.'

!

Drivers who formed a hundred-yard queue at a newly opened petrol station in Wellingborough in October 1980 to buy petrol at an introductory 50p a gallon were booked by police for illegal parking.

!

Authorities in Athens announced new regulations in November 1982 to restrict the use of private cars in the city centre in an attempt to reduce air pollution and traffic congestion. Cars with registration plates ending 1–5 were allowed into the city one day, alternating with those with numbers 6–0 on the next, and so on. A month later, a review of the scheme found that its only real effect had been to increase demand for cars by 120% as Athenians rushed to buy a second vehicle to evade the restrictions.

!

A similar scheme in New York in the late '70s, this time to save energy, forbade the use of the state's freeways by cars with only a driver. The result was a boom in the sex appliance trade as demand for inflatable rubber passengers soared.

!

A Japanese motor company was reported in 1982 to have successfully designed a substitute for petrol: tangerine oil. The only drawback, its announcement revealed, was that it took some 11,000 tangerines to produce one litre of fuel.

!

Wanderlust ... Between 26 January 1977 and 18 September 1983 Briton George Meegan walked the entire length of the American continent, from the southern tip of Tierra del Fuego to the northernmost point of Alaska, 19,021 miles away. Thought to be the longest walk in recorded history, Meegan married his wife on the way, in Argentina, and had two children born during the walk.

!

A drunken passenger arriving in Sydney from England in January 1983 was arrested after failing to answer properly routine questions from immigration officers. To the enquiry, 'Do you have a criminal record?' he is reported to have replied, 'I didn't realise it was still necessary.'

!

A Chinese theatrical troupe which returned home from a tour of Japan in 1981 was investigated for wasting China's precious foreign exchange reserves. Customs officers confiscated 69 TV sets, 30 refrigerators, 68 tape recorders, 57 cameras, 28 calculators, 138 watches and 5 electric fans.

!

An unnamed Arab prince was reported in January 1986 to have bought a forty-acre wood near Colchester for £95,000 as a once-a-year picnic spot for his family.

!

In December 1985 the Dover Chamber of Commerce invited their opposite numbers in Calais to their annual dinner. With both organisations flatly opposed to the Channel Tunnel, because of the loss of business to their ports, the occasion was seen to be an ideal opportunity to publicise jointly their views. Unfortunately, the dinner had to go ahead without the French guests. Their ferry was cancelled because of industrial action.

!

Spotted at Singapore Airport in 1982 – a luggage trolley firmly labelled 'British Rail. Not to be removed from Crewe station'.

!

The following tourist stories were all reported in the early '80s. True or apocryphal, they are offered as an antidote to the oft-held belief that travel broadens the mind. In practice it simply confuses it:

An American tourist admiring Stonehenge in 1980 was overheard to remark, 'Hasn't changed much since 1972, has it?'

!

A group of American tourists escorted around the Houses of Parliament suddenly found themselves in the presence of the then Lord Chancellor, Lord Hailsham, resplendent in full wig and gown. Spying behind the group the figure of Neil Marten MP, the Lord Chancellor called out in greeting 'Neil' with dignified vigour. And all the Americans did.

!

A tourist, again from America, on a driving holiday in Britain was reported to have been overcome by the Cotswolds but astonished at the number of villages with the same name. 'After Chipping Sodbury,' he said, 'there were three villages in a row called Loose Chippings.'

!

An English classics scholar, trying to impress his tour party colleagues on holiday in Athens, offered to converse in Greek with the local ferry officers at the docks to enquire about departure times. The locals, after recovering from fits of laughter, then revealed to the rest of the group, in perfect English, the scholar's question: 'When do the galleys sail for the Isle of Aegina, O sailors?'

!

A Birmingham hotelier fondly remembers the American guest who when asked how he would like his boiled egg replied, 'Medium rare'.

!

A guide at Windsor Castle was struggling to make herself heard over the roar of low flying aircraft coming into land at nearby Heathrow. She was interrupted by an American tourist who demanded what was wrong with the town planners and why had they built the castle so close to the airport.

!

The highlight of a cruise liner's visit to the Alaskan port of Valdez was a guided tour of the southern end of the great 800 mile pipeline through which, the guide informed them, some 1.3 million barrels of oil came daily from Prudoe Bay in the north. When he asked if there were any questions, an American solemnly enquired, 'How do they get all those empty barrels back up to Prudoe Bay?'

!

An elderly man who had never been to London took up the offer of a day out there. He sat silently throughout, staring at the vast crowds, the busy shops and the traffic. On his return home he was asked his opinion. 'If I'd known it was market day, I'd never have gone,' he replied.

!

A Hungarian who had been allowed to emigrate was asked which country he wanted to go to. He couldn't make up his mind and was handed a large globe to help. After further intense study, he said, 'Do you have another globe?'

!

A competition among air travelling executives for the worst experience of 1985 was won by a passenger on an internal Nigerian Airlines flight which had been over-booked three times. The control crew's solution to the problem was to require all prospective passengers to run twice round the aircraft, the fastest third qualifying for the seats.

!

Don't try to land in northern Portugal unless it's in school hours. Air traffic authorities had to suspend flights to the regional centre of Viseu in March 1981 after the runway became a popular venue for children to play. One incoming aircraft had to abort its landing and nearly collided with a tractor in a nearby field. Local children told police that their parents had banned them from playing in the streets because of the danger of traffic.

!

In 1981, fifty San Francisco nudists arrived in Miami for a national convention to find their airline had lost all their luggage, including their clothes.

!

The 1982 Association of British Travel Agents confer-ence in Phoenix, Arizona, had to change its venue at the last moment when it discovered that its original hotel had been double booked.

!

British Airways' special tours for staff in 1981 included a honeymoon trip to the West Indian island of St Lucia. 'Prices,' it added, 'are based on four/five people sharing.'

!

The hotel industry survives by pandering to their guests' every need. Some however are less than perfect in communicating their assets, as the following reports from around the world illustrate:

'Please do not use the lift when it is not working.'

'To call room service, please to open door and call "Room Service".'

'Steaks and chops are grilled before our customers.'

'A doctor is ever present to give the best attention. He has all the diseases at his fingertips.'

'Ladies are requested not to have children in the cocktail room.'

'This is an inexpensive all-in hotel for the family. No tax, no tips, no service.'

'In the hotel restaurant the waitress will give you a bill and you may sign her on the back side.'

'A resort for people seeking real peace and quiet. Fine hotels, gourmet food and all the time in the world to be undisturbed. So if you want to get away from it all, come and see us. Every year over 85,000 visitors come to enjoy the solitude.'

'Restaurant open. Haute and cold cuisine.'

'Spend your honeymoon with us and we'll guarantee you'll say it's the best honeymoon you've ever had.'

'Sun and snooze after a luscious gourmet lunch. Then climb on the high board and dive into our king size pool. We fill it with water every day.'

'This is a comfortable and friendly family hotel in a superb position on the promenade. Children love it because, unlike some resorts, the sea comes right up to the shore.'

'In case of fire do not panic your self. Our staffs will do all that is necessary.'

!

# FIFTEEN

# **LAST WORDS**

To round off, a miscellany of one hundred and one wise, witty but mostly silly sayings of the recent past:

'Nice to see you again, Mr Ambassador.'
Ronald Reagan greeting, for the first time, Denis Healey,
Labour Foreign Affairs spokesman, March 1987

'Politics is like a high mountain. Only eagles and reptiles get to the top.'
Northern Ireland MP, March 1988

'No one would have remembered the Good Samaritan if he'd only had good intentions. He had money as well.'
Margaret Thatcher, 1980

'The "dynamic benefits" Britain has enjoyed through membership of the EEC can be compared to UFOs: a lot of people talk about them, precious few people claim to have seen them, and those who have are doubted.'
W D Hickson, *Guardian*, March 1979

'I do not see the EEC as a great love affair. It is more like nine middle-aged couples with failing marriages meeting at a Brussels hotel for a group grope.'
Kenneth Tynan, 1975

'I understand that Camden Council, for example, discriminates against certain sorts of graffiti. A ratepayer telephoned recently to ask for the removal of the slogan "Kilroy was here". He was told that it would not be possible to have that removed. He then inquired further and was told that if the graffiti had said "Kilroy was queer" the Council would remove it.'

Christopher Chope, Environment Minister,
House of Commons, December 1986


'He is a very, very skilful politician. He knows when to keep quiet.'

Margaret Thatcher on Tony Benn, May 1979


'The Marxist analysis has got nothing to do with what happened in Stalin's Russia: it's like blaming Jesus Christ for the Inquisition in Spain.'

Tony Benn, 1980


'I don't mind how much my ministers talk – as long as they do what I say.'

Margaret Thatcher, 1987


'I'll always be fond of dear Ted, but there's no sympathy in politics.'

Margaret Thatcher, on becoming Tory leader, February
1975


'It's a pity others had to leave theirs on the ground at Goose Green to prove it.'

Neil Kinnock, responding to a heckler who
said Mrs Thatcher 'had guts'. Election 1983

'Landslides, on the whole, don't produce successful governments.'

Francis Pym, election 1983

'I think I can handle a landslide majority all right.'

Margaret Thatcher, election 1983

'It is not the main thrust of my belief that we are likely to form the next government.'

David Owen, SDP leader, election 1983

'Opinion polls are like bikinis: what they reveal is interesting, but what they conceal is vital.'

Len Murray, TUC, 1980

'The Russians are praying for a Labour victory.'

Denis Healey, opening day of election campaign, 1987

'Somebody ought to tell Denis that the Russians don't pray.'

David Owen, second day of election campaign, 1987

'The price of oil is not determined by the British Parliament. It is determined by some lads riding camels who do not even know how to spell national sovereignty.'

Lord Feather, 1975

'An Iranian moderate is one who has run out of ammunition.'

Henry Kissinger, 1987

'When I go down to the House of Lords the only way I can keep awake is by making a speech myself. Otherwise it is almost impossible: it is so soporific down there.'

Lord Shinwell, 1975

'The (Opposition) Member for Ipswich criticised some of the additions to the Bill that were made in the House of Lords ... (He) used the term "backwoodsmen" ... It is much better to come from the backwoods than the avant garden.'

Chris Patten, Education Minister, Education Bill Committee, June 1986

'Asking Neil Kinnock to give a brief answer to a brief question is like trying to get a drink of water from a burst water main.'

Norman Tebbit, 1987

'He didn't riot. He got on his bike and looked for work.'

Norman Tebbit, on his father's attitude to unemployment, Conservative Party conference, October 1981

'But I mustn't go on singling out names ... One must not be a name dropper as Her Majesty reminded me only yesterday.'

Norman St John Stevas, Arts Minister, Museum of the Year Awards, 1979

'I used to say that politics was the second oldest profession, and I have come to know that it bears a gross similarity to the first.'

Ronald Reagan, election campaign, 1980

'Well, I suppose when you have been in the jungle for a few years shooting people it is a bit difficult to understand.'

New Zealand PM Robert Muldoon, in debate with Zimbabwe PM Robert Mugabe, Commonwealth Conference, Melbourne, 1981

'He should go and find himself a good taxidermist.'
New Zealand PM Robert Muldoon on Nigerian
President Shagari, Commonwealth Conference,
Melbourne 1981

'You're from what?'
New Zealand PM Robert Muldoon to a journalist who
introduced himself as "from Bangladesh",
Commonwealth Conference, Melbourne, 1981

'We utter millions of words, fill reams of paper, notes, reports, resolutions and communiques, most of which have no subsequent impact, consume lavish meals, listen to flowery oratory … enable the globetrotting journalist to massage his ego and then go home, presumably with the feeling of a job well done.'
New Zealand PM Robert Muldoon,
verdict on Commonwealth Conference, Melbourne, 1981

'He is a bull carrying his own china shop.'
Inder Jit, Indian editor,
on Robert Muldoon, Melbourne 1981

'Influence is like a savings account. The less you use it, the more you've got.'
Andrew Young, US Ambassador to UN, 1977

'If you've got 'em by the balls, their hearts and minds will follow.'
Sign on Nixon aide Chuck Colson's desk,
White House, 1972

'You can believe me. I'm not smart enough to lie.'
Ronald Reagan, 1980

'It is never wise to try to appear to be more clever than you are. It is sometimes wise to appear slightly less so.'

William Whitelaw MP, 1975

'I have difficulty looking humble for extended periods of time.'

Henry Kissinger, 1981

'The more angry I get, the more clothes I take off.'
Ilona Staller, 'Cicciolina' porn star elected member of Italian Parliament for Radical Party, July 1987

'My fellow Americans. I am pleased to tell you that I have just signed legislation to outlaw Russia for ever. We begin bombing in five minutes.'
Ronald Reagan testing microphone for radio address, 11 August 1984

'Where there is discord, may we bring harmony,
Where there is error, may we bring truth,
Where there is doubt, may we bring faith,
Where there is despair, may we bring hope.'
Margaret Thatcher, on taking office, 4 May 1979

'It is fatal in life to be right too soon.'
Enoch Powell, March 1979

'We do not inherit the countryside from our fathers but borrow it from our children.'
Ecology Party election slogan, 1979

'You have got to give this much to the Luftwaffe – when it knocked down our buildings, it did not replace them with anything more offensive than rubble. We did that.'
Prince Charles, on modern architecture, 1987

'In the days when the nation depended on agriculture for its wealth, it made the Lord Chancellor sit on a woolsack to remind him where the wealth came from. I would like to suggest we remove that now and make him sit on a crate of machine tools.'

Prince Philip, launching Industry Year, July 1986

'Seen one Redwood, you've seen 'em all.'

Ronald Reagan, on ecology

'What a terrible revenge for Pearl Harbour.'

S I Hayakawa, Japanese industrialist, on the success of McDonalds in Tokyo

'Americans have the best system in the world: they've just got to find a way to make it work.'

Vice-President Nelson Rockefeller, 1975

'Sometimes when I look at my children, I say to myself, "Lillian, you should have stayed a virgin".'

Lillian Carter, mother of President Jimmy, 1980

'It's true hard work never killed anybody, but I figure why take the chance.'

Ronald Reagan, March 1987

'It was easier for a camel to go through the eye of a needle than for a rich man to get into the Kingdom of Heaven, so if the rich are taxed more heavily at least it would be partially for their own good.'

Ivor Clemitson MP, 1975

'We have no political prisoners. We have political internal exiles.'

President Augusto Pinochet of Chile, 1975

'The time to start complaining is when you can see hammers and sickles on their wings.'

> Reply from RAF Leuchars, Fife, to resident complaining about aircraft flying so low she could see their markings, March 1987

'Keep quiet at the back – statistically you've got most to lose.'

> Retort of BA shuttle stewardess demonstrating safety procedures, 1986

'Ladies and gentlemen, this is your captain speaking. We have a small problem and all four engines have stopped. We are all doing our damndest to get them working again. I trust you are not in too much distress.'

> Eric Moody, BA 747 captain, reporting to his passengers, July 1982
> (The engines restarted 90 seconds later)

'Science has conquered many diseases, broken the genetic code and even placed human beings on the moon, yet when a man of eighty is left in a room with two eighteen-year-old cocktail waitresses, nothing happens. Because the real problems never change.'

> Woody Allen, 1981

'It's funny. When you speak to God it's called praying; but when God speaks to you, it's called schizophrenia.'

> Psychiatrist commenting on trial of Yorkshire Ripper, May 1981

'I think that a judge should be looked on rather as a sphinx than as a person – you shouldn't be able to imagine a judge having a bath.'

> Judge H C Leon, 1975

'Jesus is coming, and Boy! is he pissed off.'
Placard of evangelist David McKay, arrested in Mildura,
Australia, March 1982. He said in mitigation to the
court that his slogans encouraged young people to take
an interest in God.

'Drop Kick Me Jesus Through the Goalposts of Life.'
Hit ballad, Texan religious radio station, 1982

'We've all got to die sometime.'
Magistrate James Hobson Jobling, Horseferry Road
Court, London, November 1985, responding to
mitigation plea for drink-drive woman who had been
told she only had six months to live

'I intend to open the country up to democracy and
anyone who is against that I will jail, I will crush.'
President Joao Figueiredo of Brazil, on inauguration,
1979

'A nuclear power plant is infinitely safer than eating
because 300 people choke to death on food every year.'
Dixie Lee Ray, Governor of Washington state, 1977

'You can't have a race living here for 70,000 years
without leaving some of their debris about. In another
70,000 years you will be able to see our beer cans, won't
you, as a sign of our culture.'
Australian Minister for Conservation
on Aboriginal artifacts, December 1981

'I'm not a criminal. I'm an ex-crook.'
Ronald Biggs, 1981

'The time for balloting is over. It is time to stand up and be counted.'

Jack Taylor, President Yorkshire miners, January 1983

'There's no point in going on strike. We've got such a poor service, the public would hardly miss it.'

Terry Allen, London bus union official, during 'winter of discontent', February 1979

'We've got to be seen to be getting our retaliation in first.'

South Wales NUM official, miners' strike, 1985

'I don't want to be quoted and don't quote me that I don't want to be quoted.'

Winston Burdett, CBS TV, 1981

'A condom on the penis of progress.'

Ian Tuxworth, Production Minister, Northern Territory, Australia, on the national airline, QANTAS, July 1983

'My, you must have fun chasing the soap round the bath.'

Princess of Wales, shaking hands with one-armed man during Australian tour, June 1983

'At least I only left shoes in my cupboard, not skeletons. And besides, I didn't have 3,000 pairs of shoes. I only had 1,060.'

Imelda Marcos, in exile, 1987

'Ghengis Khan was not exactly lovable but I suppose he is my favourite historical character because he was damned efficient.'

Kerry Packer, media entrepreneur, 1979

'Where would Christianity be if Jesus had got eight to fifteen years with time off for good behaviour?'

> New York senator James Donovan
> supporting capital punishment, April 1978

'We should declare war on North Vietnam. We could pave the whole country and put parking stripes on it, and still be home by Christmas.'

> Ronald Reagan, 1966

'If the only tool you have is a hammer, you tend to see every problem as a nail.'

> Abraham Maslow, 1981

'My nets shrank.'

> Robert Arensman, Dutch trawlerman,
> unsuccessfully explaining his undersized mesh
> to a North Shields court, January 1986

'Neil Armstrong was the first man to walk on the Moon. I'm the first man to piss his pants on the Moon.'

> Buzz Aldrin, 1970

'Owing to our coverage of the French Open tennis championships, "The Invisible Man" will not be seen tonight.'

> Continuity announcer, Channel 9, Melbourne 1983

'Of course Kirkpatrick will serve nowhere near the 900 years to which he has been sentenced because the system in Northern Ireland allows for up to 50% remission for good behaviour.'

> Northern Ireland reporter, Radio 4 News, June 1983

'Don't worry if you're not listening now as the programme will be repeated tomorrow evening.'

Radio 2 announcer, 1985

'Sarah Brightman couldn't act scared on the New York subway at four o'clock in the morning.'

Joel Segal, ABC, reviewing *Phantom of the Opera*, January 1988

'Some people think football is a matter of life and death. I don't like that attitude. I can assure them it is much more serious than that.'

Bill Shankly, Liverpool manager, 1973

'At first we thought there was a truce, then we discovered the militiamen were watching the game. Since then we have had a few quiet hours every night.'

Beirut resident during Mexico World Cup, 1986

'I resigned as a coach because of illness and fatigue. The fans were sick and tired of me.'

John Ralston, on resigning from Denver Broncos, 1978

'I just opened the trophy cabinet. Two Japanese prisoners of war came out.'

Tommy Docherty, on taking over as manager of ailing Wolverhampton Wanderers, 1985

'God has a task for each of us, and you just have to do the best you can at it. For me, right now, it just happens to be running a marathon backwards.'

Albert Freese, world backwards marathon record holder, 1985

'You can stop counting, I'm not getting up.'
Jim Watt, former world lightweight boxing champion,
suggesting his epitaph, 1985

'Before the race, people ask you if you're going to win, and it's impossible to say; but after the race it's a little easier.'
Alain Prost, 1985

'I'm still chasing the girls but now I'm catching them.'
Sports Council youth promotion slogan, 1985

'Bloody hell, Ma'am, what's he doing in here?'
Buckingham Palace chambermaid discovering Michael
Fagan in the Queen's bedroom, July 1982

'The real lesson of this incident is that women of all social classes are vulnerable to attack by men.'
*Labour Herald* on Royal intruder incident, 1982

'To President Figueiredo and the people of Bolivia ... I mean Brazil. Bolivia's where I'm going next.'
Ronald Reagan, toasting his host in Brasilia,
December 1982. His next stop was Colombia.
Bolivia was not on the itinerary.

'... a great man who should have been President and would have been one of the greatest Presidents in history – Hubert Horatio Hornblower ... er Humphrey.'
President Jimmy Carter, 1980 Democratic Convention,
paying tribute to the recently deceased party elder
statesman

'A woman rang to say that she'd heard there was a hurricane on the way. Well, don't worry. There isn't.'
BBC weatherman Michael Fish on the eve of the 'Great Storm', October 1987

'The Olympic movement appears as a ray of sunshine through clouds of racial animosity, religious bigotry and political chicanery.'
Avery Brundage, President International Olympic Committee, 1972, before the Munich massacre, the African boycott of Montreal, the Western boycott of Moscow and the eastern boycott of Los Angeles

'I feel a degree of regret that Marshall did not push on and say 'abolish the GLC' because I think it would have been a major saving and would have released massive resources for more productive use.'
Ken Livingstone, 1979, when an Opposition Labour councillor, on the 1977 Marshall report on the future of the GLC

'At various times in the next twenty or thirty years I think it is reasonable to anticipate that I will be among the leadership of the Labour Party, but as for being leader, I can't see it happening, and I'm not particularly keen on it happening.'
Neil Kinnock, January 1981

'We will make them grovel.'
Tony Greig, English cricket captain, before 1976 Test series against West Indies – England lost 3–0

'Tourists go home from my constituency with their photographs showing them with one foot in the northern hemisphere and one in the southern.'

Greenwich MP Rosie Barnes' maiden speech, House of Commons, March 1987

'To the great people and the Government of Israel ... excuse me – of Egypt.'

President Gerald Ford, toasting his host President Sadat at official dinner, Cairo, 1975

'He probably spends two or three hours at most on real work. There are times when you really need him to do some work and all he wants to do is tell stories about his movie days.'

Aide to Ronald Reagan, August 1981, eight months into office

'He doesn't make snap decisions, but he doesn't tend to overthink either.'

Nancy Reagan, on Ronald, 1980

'I would expect things to go on much as they are until there is some change.'

Sir Anthony Parsons, diplomat, assessing Iran-Iraq war, 1984

!